UNIQUE
Georgia

A Guide to the State's Quirks, Charisma, and Character

Tom Barr

John Muir Publications
Santa Fe, New Mexico

Special thanks to Albany-Dougherty County Chamber of Commerce; Andersonville National Historic Site; Athens Convention and Visitors Bureau; Atlanta Convention and Visitors Bureau; Augusta-Richmond County Convention and Visitors Bureau; Brunswick and the Golden Isles Visitors Bureau; Carroll County Chamber of Commerce; Cartersville-Bartow County Convention and Visitors Bureau; Cherokee County Chamber of Commerce; Chickamauga and Chattanooga National Military Park; Clayton County Convention and Visitors Bureau; Cobb County Convention and Visitors Bureau; Columbus Convention and Visitors Bureau; Dalton Convention and Visitors Bureau; DeKalb Convention and Visitors Bureau; Destination Thomasville Tourism Authority; Equitable Real Estate Investment Management, Inc.; Fernbank Museum of Natural History; Gainesville Hall County Convention and Visitors Bureau; Georgia Department of Industry, Trade and Tourism; Georgia Department of Natural Resources-State Parks, Wildlife Divisions; Georgia Poultry Federation, Inc.; Georgia's Stone Mountain Park; Greater Rome Convention and Visitors Bureau; Historic Roswell Convention and Visitors Bureau; Jekyll Island Authority; Macon-Bibb County Convention and Visitors Bureau, Inc.; Madison-Morgan County Chamber of Commerce; Marietta Welcome Center and Visitors Bureau; Martin Luther King Jr. National Historic Site; Okefenokee National Wildlife Refuge; Peanut Advisory Board; Piedmont National Wildlife Refuge; Pine Mountain Tourism Association, Inc.; Plains Peanuts; Savannah Area Convention and Visitors Bureau; Underground Atlanta; U.S. Fish and Wildlife Service-Savannah Coastal Refuges; Valdosta-Lowndes County Convention and Visitors Bureau; Waycross-Ware County Chamber of Commerce.

John Muir Publications, P.O. Box 613, Santa Fe, New Mexico 87504
© 1995 by Tom Barr
Cover © 1995 by John Muir Publications
All rights reserved. Published 1995
Printed in the United States of America

First edition. First printing September 1995.

Library of Congress Cataloging-in-Publication Data
Barr, Tom
Unique Georgia: a guide to the state's quirks, charisma, and character / Tom Barr.
    p. cm.
    Includes index.
    ISBN 1-56261-240-9 (pbk.)
    1. Georgia—Guidebooks. 2. Georgia—Miscellanea. I. Title.
F284.3.B37 1995
917.5804'43—dc20   95-7321
                                                             CIP

Front cover photo: Leo de Wys, Inc./Stan Ries
Back cover photo: Leo de Wys, Inc./Everett C. Johnson
Editors: Elizabeth Wolf, Dianna Delling
Copy editor: Heidi Utz
Production: Kathryn Lloyd-Strongin, Janine Lehmann
Typesetting: Marcie Pottern
Illustrations: Maria Voris, Bette Brodsky
Printer: Malloy Lithographing, Inc.

Distributed to the book trade by
Publishers Group West
Emeryville, California

CONTENTS

INTRODUCTION

Nothing but green forests, Civil War battlefields, antebellum architecture, and blue skies. That's Georgia, right? Take a skylift ride to the summit of Stone Mountain, canoe through the mysterious Okefenokee Swamp, raft the surging white waters of the Wild and Scenic Chattooga River, or bask in the sun on the Golden Isles, and you know you couldn't be any place but Georgia. In Georgia you'll also find graceful waterfalls, the nation's oldest military park, birthplaces of civil rights leaders and rock 'n' roll stars, stately plantations, and former pleasure palaces of the rich and famous.

Georgia's northern mountains offer graceful waterfalls, rugged rock formations, and endless forested vistas

Of course, there are still many other things to discover about unique Georgia. For example, while it ranks 21st in size, it is the largest state east of the Mississippi River. Did you know that forest covers two-thirds of Georgia, that its 100 miles of shoreline harbor some of the nation's most unique wildlife, and that its waters once yielded the record largemouth bass? Did you know that, in Georgia, you can retrace Sherman's march to the sea, follow the route of the Great Locomotive Chase, discover revolutionary war battlefields, and walk along a seashore where Sir Francis Drake and Blackbeard the Pirate raided enemy ships? Or that Georgia festivals celebrate everything from wildlife to barbecue, from steeplechases to horse-and-buggy races, from Confederate history to ethnic heritages?

Unique Georgia presents fascinating facts, intriguing destinations, tantalizing trivia, handy charts, and quick access maps in a user-friendly format. Where else can you find recipes for chicken pita, Chatham Artillery Punch, and Brunswick Stew; the best places to watch wildlife; and tips for off-the-beaten-path recreation?

Tourist Division, Georgia Dept. of Industry and Trade

However you choose to use this book, you'll soon find out what is unique about the state of Georgia.

Life in a Live Oak

Georgia's state tree is known for its hard wood, enormous size, and huge twisting, winding limbs. The frigate *Constitution,* known as "Old Ironsides," and the Brooklyn Bridge were built of Georgia live oaks. While live oaks live an average of 300 years, some last much longer. Thomasville's Big Oak, dating to 1685, stands 68 feet high and 24 feet in circumference, with limbs spanning 162 feet. Depending on the environment, live oaks provide rich habitat for a variety of wildlife. Spanish moss drapes the high branches, while wild grapevines wind around trunks and lower limbs. Acorns and grapes provide autumn forage for black bear, deer, wild turkey, alligators, and snapping turtles. Songbirds, bobcats, brown bats, great horned owls, and flying squirrels nest and rest in the limbs. At Albany's **Tift Park**, you can follow a "carriage trail" through an archway of 58 live oak trees which were planted in 1912. *FYI:* 1300 N. Monroe, Albany.

Georgia

Population:
6,623,000

Area:
58,876 sq. miles

State Capital: Atlanta

Nicknames:
The Peach State
Empire State of the
South

Date of Statehood:
January 2, 1788

Highest Elevation:
Brasstown Bald
Mountain
4,784 ft.

State Tree: Live oak

State Flower:
Cherokee rose

State Bird:
Brown thrasher

State Fish:
Largemouth bass

State Fossil:
Shark tooth

State Song:
"Georgia on My Mind"

THEN AND NOW

10,000 B.C.-A.D. 1500

Approximately 10,000 years ago Georgia was inhabited mostly by alligators, mastodons, and other wildlife. No one knows where the first people came from, or when they arrived. As the last Ice Age glaciers melted, hunters may have followed their food supply south to Georgia. For thousands of years, they subsisted by hunting deer and turkey, gathering wild plants and berries, and catching shellfish, shad, and sturgeon. During much of the year, they roamed the landscape taking advantage of seasonal food supplies. By 2000 B.C. they had learned to make pottery.

About A.D. 900 a more sophisticated culture, which originated in the Mississippi Valley, moved into the Macon area. Dubbed the "Mississippian culture" by archaeologists, their lifestyle was based in agriculture. Soon corn, beans, squash, tobacco, and pumpkins sprouted from bottomlands. These crops supported towns of 500 to 1,000 inhabitants, who lived in rectangular houses plastered with clay and covered by thatched roofs. They carved stone pipes, wore shell jewelry, and made intricate sculptures and masks. Nearby they built circular earth lodges and large flat-topped mounds, which may have been used for sun worshipping or burying the dead. They held sophisticated religious beliefs and developed extensive trading networks.

Gradually the cultures intermingled and coexisted for several centuries. Around A.D. 1500 they stopped building mounds and eventually disappeared. Archaeologists speculate that they may have died of disease, been conquered by warlike tribes which invaded the area around A.D. 1000, or been assimilated into the Creek Indian nation.

Several sites preserve remnants of prehistoric Indian cultures:

1) Etowah Indian Mounds: Between A.D. 1000 and 1500, these mounds were the ceremonial center for a community of several thousand people. The largest is 63 feet tall and covers three acres. It

Excavations at Etowah Indian Mounds have yielded artifacts thousands of years old

Tourist Division, Georgia Dept. of Industry and Trade

Indian Sites

may have been a priest's temple. Effigy figures, copper ear ornaments, shell jewelry, and other museum artifacts indicate an extensive trade network, since some materials exist only in regions hundreds of miles away. *FYI:* 813 Indian Mounds Rd., S.W., Cartersville; (404) 387-3747.

2) **Fort Mountain State Park:** The thick, prehistoric, man-made defense wall, extending 855 feet around the mountain's crest, is believed to have been made by Indians more than 1,000 years ago as a ceremonial center or fortification. *FYI:* Seven miles east of Chatsworth; (706) 695-2621.

3) **Kolomoki Mounds:** Georgia's oldest great temple mound was an important population center. Designated a National Historic Landmark, these seven mounds were built in the 12th and 13th centuries. Kolomoki Mounds Museum exhibits an intact small burial mound. *FYI:* Blakely; (912) 723-5296.

4) **Ocmulgee National Monument:** The largest archaeological development east of the Mississippi documents 12,000 years of Native American culture and heritage with earth lodges, mounds, tools, and weapons. Trails lead to mounds that were part of a town dating from A.D. 900–1100. *FYI:* 1207 Emory Hwy., Macon; (912) 752-8257.

5) **Rock Eagle Mound:** The mound is believed to be more than 5,000 years old. Made of rocks shaped like an eagle, it stretches 120 feet from wingtip to wingtip and 102 feet from head to tail. *FYI:* U.S. 129 and 441, Eatonton; (404) 485-2831.

Etowah Indian Mounds

Georgia State Parks

Three Flags Over Georgia

Hernando De Soto was the first European to explore Georgia. In March 1540 he and 600 men spent four months in Georgia on a fruitless search for gold. His expedition captured and killed local Indians and recorded North America's first Christian baptism near Ocmulgee. After De Soto, many Indians died from smallpox and measles.

During the next two centuries, Spain, France, and England claimed Georgia. Spain ruled from 1565 into the 1700s. They ousted the French and named the area "Guale," in honor of a friendly Indian chief.

England claimed Georgia in 1629, but waited nearly a century before establishing Fort King George on the Altamaha River as the southernmost frontier of the British Empire in North America. In the interim pirates used Georgia's islands as a base for raiding Spanish galleons.

Georgia's Father

In 1729 James Oglethorpe, a member of the British Parliament, had a bright idea: instead of debtors rotting in English prisons, they could colonize the new world. He petitioned King George II to grant land between South Carolina and Florida. Appealing to the king's ego, he suggested that it be named "Georgia" in his honor. The settlement would also assure that the land between Florida and the Carolinas was settled by the English, thus offering a convenient location for monitoring Spanish action in Florida and French activities in Louisiana.

James Oglethorpe

As England's only contribution to an American colony, parliament anteed up 10,000 pounds to support the enterprise. On June 9, 1732, King George II created the last of the 13 colonies by granting a charter for a corporation called "the Trustees for Establishing the Colony of Georgia in America."

Oglethorpe was named the trustees' agent and, in effect, Georgia's first governor. Unlike in other colonies, slavery and importation of hard liquors were prohibited, and the 21 trustees who were to administer the colony could not own land or profit from the enterprise.

On February 12, 1733—celebrated thereafter as Georgia Day—Oglethorpe and 35 families landed at the mouth of the Savannah River and laid out the first town, Savannah.

The founders did not limit their colony either to the poor or to Englishmen, and fewer than 2,000 charity cases ever reached Georgia. By 1740 parties of Germans, Swiss, Piedmont Italians, Jews, and Welsh had arrived.

Fort Frederica National Monument

Strategically, Frederica was the most important of Georgia's early settlements. Its purpose was to monitor the Spanish and assert Britain's claim to Georgia's coast. Built in 1736 and named after Frederick Louis, the settlement was garrisoned by 500 to 1,000 people, who maintained strict discipline and daily military drills. After threats to Georgia's coast declined, Frederica disbanded in 1749. Ruins of the fort, barracks, and homes still stand. *FYI:* Frederica Rd., St. Marys; (912) 638-3639.

Fort Frederica

The War of Jenkins' Ear

Spain considered Georgia's settlers trespassers. Their hatred intensified as England violated trade agreements by smuggling cargo to Spanish possessions off the Florida coast.

A revolutionary war battle is reenacted at Fort King George

In retaliation, Spain seized British ships and punished British seamen. When they caught English smuggler Robert Jenkins in 1730, they confiscated his cargo and allegedly cut off one of his ears. Jenkins saved his ear and, when he showed it to the British Parliament in 1739, it precipitated a war lasting five years. With Georgia at the center of the conflict, Oglethorpe led several expeditions into Florida, capturing Spanish forts and destroying ships.

Battle of Bloody Marsh

On July 7, 1742, Spain attacked Frederica with 50 ships and 2,800 to 4,000 men. Oglethorpe's 650 defenders won the battle by attacking the invaders while they rested beside a marsh, and turned the ground red with Spanish blood. Afterwards, Spain never made another serious effort to occupy Georgia.

Life in the Georgia colony was anything but a Garden of Eden. The prohibitions regarding ownership of land, slaves, and liquor were so unpopular that many defected to South Carolina. After the rules were rescinded in 1850, thousands migrated to Georgia. When the trustees returned the corporate charter to England in 1752, Georgia became the fastest growing royal colony.

American Revolution

When England won the French and Indian War, Georgia was freed from the threat of Spain and France, and could claim territory as far west as the Mississippi River. But England expected colonists to help repay its war debt. Without consulting them, it levied taxes on tea and other imports.

Georgia was only 40 years old when the Revolution began. It was the only colony that allowed imports to be taxed within its borders. Many of its colonists had been born in England and remained loyal to the mother country.

In the Battle of Rice Boats, fought in March 1776 at Savannah, Americans burned ships and the British took about 1,600 barrels of rice. Americans won at Fort Morris and at Kettle Creek, but by the spring of 1780 the British had seized everything in Georgia except a small section near Augusta. **Fort Morris Historic Site** contains revolutionary war earthwork fortifications, a museum, and walking tour. *FYI:* Midway; (912) 884-5999.

One of the worst American defeats in the Revolution occurred on October 9, 1779, when the colonists attempted to recapture

Only 40 years old when the Revolution began, Georgia was the fourth state to join the Union, in 1788

New Hampshire
Massachusetts
New York
Rhode Island
Connecticut
Pennsylvania
New Jersey
Delaware
Maryland
Virginia
North Carolina
South Carolina
Georgia

Savannah. The 90-minute battle saw 1,000 of 4,000 attackers killed. Polish Count Casimir Pulaski, who had come to America to fight for freedom, was killed leading a valiant cavalry charge. Fort Pulaski, now a national monument, was named in his honor.

In June 1782, General "Mad" Anthony Wayne won Georgia's last revolutionary war battle and forced the British out a year before Americans won independence. On January 2, 1788, Georgia became the fourth state to join the Union. **The Signers Monument** was erected in 1848, as a memorial to the three Georgia signers of the Declaration of Independence: George Walton, Lyman Hall, and Button Gwinnett. *FYI:* 500 Greene St., Augusta.

Eli Whitney

Eli Whitney

In 1793 Whitney was serving as a tutor on General Nathanael Greene's plantation near Savannah. Greene's widow asked him to design a machine that would remove seeds from cotton fibers. Whitney built his cotton gin in six months and claimed it removed seeds 50 times faster than by hand. Production increased from 1,000 to 150,000 bales per year and made Georgia the world's largest cotton grower. **Augusta Cotton Exchange Building**, constructed in 1886, was headquarters for 200 cotton farmers, brokers, and buyers. A museum traces cotton farming production. *FYI:* 32 Eighth St. at Riverwalk, Augusta; (706) 724-4067.

Indian Nations

By the time the mound builders disappeared and the first explorers came to Georgia, the Creek Indians had become the region's dominant tribe. The English named them "Creeks," because they often lived near streams.

Later, Cherokee Indians moved into Georgia's Appalachian Highlands. Originally cave dwellers, they developed their own schools, organized an independent government, and wrote a constitution. In 1825 they established New Echota in northwest Georgia. It was the capital and seat of government for an Indian nation that covered northern Georgia, parts of North Carolina, Tennessee, and Alabama.

In 1821, Chief Sequoya developed an 86-character Cherokee alphabet, which was used to print North America's only bilingual Indian language newspaper

Trail of Tears

In 1838 some 15,000 Cherokees were forcibly marched to Oklahoma on what survivors called *Nunna-da-ul-tsun-yi*—the Trail of Tears. More than 8,000 Cherokees died from disease and exposure on the 2,000-mile march, which began at Dalton, Georgia.

The 150-mile-long **Chieftains Trail** was designated by the Georgia state assembly as part of the 150th anniversary of the Trail of Tears. *FYI:* (706) 295-5576 for brochures. It includes **New Echota**'s newspaper office, court building, and ruins of the Indian settlement. *FYI:* 1211 Chatsworth Hwy., N.E., Calhoun; (706) 629-8151. **Dahlonega Courthouse Gold Museum** (which is not a part of the Chieftains Trail) interprets 160 years of prospecting history and exhibits some of the $6 million coined at Dahlonega's U.S. Mint between 1838 and 1861. *FYI:* Public Square, Dahlonega; (706) 864-2257. **Chief Vann House State Historic Site** is a Federal style brick mansion built in 1804 by Chief James Vann and the showplace of the Cherokee nation. *FYI:* Three miles west of Chatsworth; (706) 695-2598.

America's First Gold Rush
When gold was discovered in 1827 at Dahlonega, it precipitated America's first gold rush and the end of the Cherokee nation. As their lands were overrun, Cherokees hired lawyers and took their legal battle to the U. S. Supreme Court, which decided in their favor. President Andrew Jackson ignored the ruling and, on May 28, 1830, signed the Indian Removal Act into law.

Civil War

On January 19, 1861, Georgia became the fifth state to secede from the Union and join ten other southern states in the Confederacy. Although Georgia congressman Alexander H. Stephens was a strict Unionist and voted against secession, he felt honor-bound to side with the South. He was named Vice President of the Confederate States.

Civilians throughout Georgia backed the rebellion with money, food, labor, and lives. Factories in Athens, Augusta, Columbus, and Macon manufactured guns, sabers, and other military equipment. Atlanta's railroads became Georgia's greatest munitions and supply center.

Library of Congress LC-BH 82-1979

General William Tecumseh Sherman, 1820–1891

Georgia's geographic location saved it from invasion during the war's early years. Union General Sherman burned Atlanta in 1864, forcing the Confederates to retreat and leaving only 400 of 3,800 buildings standing. The next day Sherman and his 62,000 men began their march to the sea. Along a path 60 miles wide and 300 miles long, his men destroyed 317 miles of railroad and $100 million worth of property, as they raided and burned farms, towns, factories, mills, and bridges. On December 22, 1864, Sherman captured Savannah and wired President Lincoln, "I beg to present you as a Christmas Gift, the City of Savannah . . ."

The Civil War continued until April 1865. During the final days, President Jefferson Davis fled Richmond, held his last cabinet meeting at Washington, Georgia, and was captured by Union Cavalry at Irwinville on May 10, 1865. Union soldiers captured Confederate Vice President Stephens at his Crawfordville estate and imprisoned him for six months. **Alexander H. Stephens State Historic Park** includes his home, Liberty Hall. It is adjacent to a **Confederate Museum**, with one of the state's best Civil War collections. *FYI:* Park St., Crawfordville; (706) 456-2602.

Jefferson Davis Memorial Park, site of his capture, is located eight miles west of Ocilla, Georgia

Library of Congress LC-USF 34-6697-D

The Great Locomotive Chase

On April 12, 1862, Union spy James Andrews and 21 Ohio soldiers disguised as civilians stole the locomotive, *General*, and three box cars at Big Shanty Station. They planned to burn all bridges and cut telegraph lines north to Chattanooga, thus isolating the important communications center. The *General*'s conductor and three crewmen chased them on foot, by hand car, and on the steam engine, *Texas*, which they operated in reverse. Eight hours and 87 miles later, the *General* ran out of steam near Ringgold. Andrews and seven cohorts were hung in Atlanta. Six survivors received the first Congressional Medals of Honor. Andrews, a civilian, was not eligible. The *General* is displayed at **Big Shanty Museum**. *FYI:* 2829 Cherokee St., Kennesaw; (404) 427-2117. The *Texas* greets visitors in the lobby of the **Atlanta Cyclorama**. *FYI:* Grant Park, Atlanta; (404) 658-7625. Adairsville salutes the event with a Great Locomotive Chase Festival. Near **Ringgold Depot**, a monument marks the spot where Andrews' Raiders abandoned the *General* and fled on foot. *FYI:* Ooltewah Rd., two miles north of Ringgold.

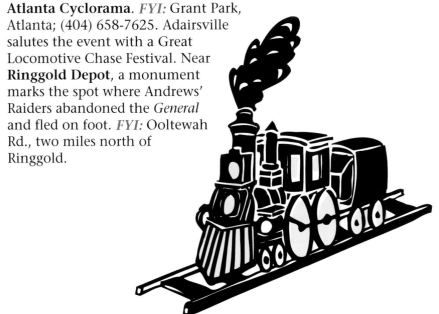

Geography of a War

Two state-designated trails include many of Georgia's Civil War sites. In Northern Georgia, **The Blue and Gray Trail** leads through battlefield parks and passes by roadside plaques, monuments, and historic cemeteries. *FYI:* (706) 629-3406 for brochure. **The Andersonville Trail** loops for 85 miles through 12 towns in central Georgia. *FYI:* (912) 928-2303.

Chickamauga National Military Park

1) Chickamauga: The first southern victory came when Yankee general William Rosecrans ordered 58,000 men into Georgia, and General Braxton Bragg massed 66,000 Confederates along winding Chickamauga Creek. On September 19 and 20, 1863, the two met in the Civil War's bloodiest two-day engagement. Combined casualties totalled over 34,000, with many killed under hand-to-hand-combat in thick woods and underbrush. Some regiments lost 55 percent of their troops.

Chickamauga-Chattanooga National Military Park, created in 1890, is the United States' oldest and largest military park. Its 8,000 acres include an eight-mile tour route and 50 miles of hiking trails.

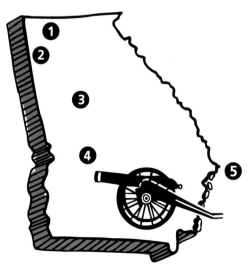

A museum features 355 weapons from the American Revolution to World War II. *FYI:* U.S. 27, Fort Oglethorpe; (706) 866-9241.

2) Lookout Mountain: On November 24, 1863, aided by a dense fog, Union soldiers forced Confederates to retreat from Lookout Mountain. The park contains monuments, historical tablets, hiking trails, and scenic vistas. *FYI:* Lookout Mountain; (706) 820-2531.

Civil War Sites

3) Kennesaw Mountain: Starting June 27, 1864, Confederates under General Joseph E. Johnston delayed Sherman's march for two weeks at Kennesaw Mountain. After losing about 3,000 men, Sherman succeeded with flanking maneuvers and continued his drive toward Atlanta. The 2,884-acre park features original earthworks and a mountaintop memorial. *FYI:* 900 Kennesaw National Dr.; (404) 427-4686.

4) Andersonville: The Civil War's most infamous prison was used for only 14 months. Up to 32,000 prisoners were crammed into 26 acres. Approximately 13,000 out of 45,000 died due to heat, poor sanitation, malnutrition, and inadequate medical care. The camp commandant, **Captain Henry Wirz**, was tried for murder and a conspiracy that never existed. Several hundred bystanders chanted, "Remember Andersonville," as he was hanged. Wirz was the only person ever executed for Civil War crimes. *FYI:* GA 49, Andersonville; (912) 924-0343.

5) Fort Pulaski National Monument: Named for revolutionary war hero Casimir Pulaski, the fort was designed by Napoleon's military engineer and built partially under the supervision of Robert E. Lee. Its fall to the Union army officially ended the era of "impregnable" masonry fortifications and verified the superiority of the rifled cannon. *FYI:* U.S. 80, east of Savannah; (912) 786-5787.

Reconstruction

Approximately 125,000 Georgians were killed in the Civil War. During reconstruction the U.S. Government ruled Georgia. Although blacks were free, there was no money to pay them. Out of this situation came sharecropping, in which landowners rented land to poor farmers in exchange for part of their crop. After Georgians ratified the

Fort Pulaski fell in April 1862, after a two-day cannon barrage

Tourist Division, Ga. Dept. of Industry & Trade

14th and 15th amendments to the Constitution, Georgia was readmitted into the United States on July 15, 1870.

Twentieth Century

Carpet Capital

One of Georgia's top industries was born near the turn of the century, when Dalton schoolgirl Catherine Evans revived the craft of tufting by copying a Colonial bedspread. Soon she and others were earning extra money making bedspreads. By the 1940s the cottage industry had expanded to scatter rugs, robes, and carpets. The billion-dollar industry made Dalton the "Carpet Capital of the World," and textiles Georgia's most important product. Today, 25 percent of the state's factory workers are employed by some 285 floor covering mills. Dalton produces approximately 65 percent of the world's carpets and has more than 100 carpet outlets offering savings of 30 to 70 percent. *FYI:* Dalton Chamber of Commerce; (706) 278-7373.

Georgia has been a leader in textiles for almost 100 years

Building a Better Bus

In 1927 A. L. Luce produced his first school bus. Today, the Blue Bird Body Company is the world's largest manufacturer of school buses. It also makes the Wanderlodge, one of the world's most luxurious recreational vehicles. The company museum houses Blue Bird Number 1 and other models. *FYI:* Fort Valley; (912) 825-2021.

Tourist Division, Ga. Dept. of Industry & Trade

The Little White House's interior remains exactly as it was on April 12, 1945, the day FDR died while vacationing here

FDR Comes to Georgia

Franklin Delano Roosevelt first came to the Pine Mountain area in 1924, seeking warm water treatments for the infantile paralysis that had stricken him at age 39. In 1932 he returned to build a six-room home for $8,738, which he called the **Little White House**. A museum displays his personal effects, including gifts from foreign embassies and his walking cane collection. Stones and flags from each of the 50 states line a garden walkway. *FYI:* Roosevelt's Little White House Historic Site, GA Hwy. 85 West, Warm Springs; (404) 655-3511.

World War II

World War II brought thousands of young Americans to train at Fort Gordon, Fort Stewart, and Fort Benning, the latter of which has become the world's largest and most modern military training center. Bell Aircraft designed, built, and tested bombers at Marietta and turned it into a major aircraft center. Brunswick's shipyards manufactured 99 cargo-carrying Liberty Ships in two years. In 1944 Savannah loaded more explosives for shipment to Europe than any American port.

National Infantry Museum: Thirty-thousand square feet are packed with infantrymen's hardware from the 17th century to the Gulf War, documents signed by U.S. presidents, captured enemy paraphernalia, paintings, and sculptures. *FYI:* Building 396 on Baltzell Ave., Fort Benning, Columbus; (706) 545-2958.

Museum of Aviation: More than 80 military aircraft are displayed. The Georgia Aviation Hall of Fame honors military and civilian aviators. *FYI:* Warner Robins Air Force Base; (912) 926-4242.

U.S. Navy Supply Corps Museum: A converted Carnegie Library building exhibits ship models, uniforms, and Navy equipment dating to the War of 1812. *FYI:* Prince and Oglethorpe Avenues, Athens; (706) 354-7349.

A 23-foot scale model of a **Liberty Ship** is located at the U.S. 17 Visitors Center in Brunswick. *FYI:* (912) 264-5337.

A memorial at **Souther Field** in Americus commemorates Charles Lindbergh's first solo flight in the single-engine *Jenny* in 1923. *FYI:* (912) 928-2303.

Civil Rights

The 20th century brought profound change to Georgia and the world. With the passage of the Civil Rights Act of 1964 and the Voting Rights Act of 1965, African Americans were guaranteed access to educational, social, economic, and political opportunities. Georgia's Andrew Young became the first black southerner in

Martin Luther King Jr. National Historic Site contains his gravesite and the Center for Nonviolent Social Change

more than 70 years to serve in the U.S. House of Representatives, and the first black U.S. ambassador to the United Nations. Atlanta turned into one of the South's most racially progressive cities. In 1973 Atlanta elected Maynard Jackson Jr. the first African American mayor of a major southern city.

Martin Luther King Jr. (1929–1968)
Atlanta-born Martin Luther King Jr. was the most eloquent and successful spokesman for racial justice. Using his philosophy of nonviolence and peaceful resistance, Dr. King and his followers staged boycotts, marches, and sit-ins in their quest for full equality. His voice was ultimately heard throughout the world, and he was awarded the 1964 Nobel Peace Prize. King was assassinated in Memphis, Tennessee, on April 4, 1968. **The Martin Luther King Jr. National Historic Site** encompasses his Queen Anne-style birthplace and the Ebenezer Baptist Church, where he and his father preached. *FYI:* 522 Auburn Ave., N.E., Atlanta; (404) 331-3920.

The Reverend Martin Luther King Jr.

Jimmy Carter

In 1976 Jimmy Carter became the first president from the Deep South since the Civil War, and the first from Georgia. The 39th president of the United States was born in Plains on October 1, 1924. A graduate of the U.S. Naval Academy, he served as a nuclear physicist before returning home to manage the family peanut farm and seed store. After a stint as state senator, he won the Georgia governor's race in 1971. An advocate of human rights, he works with Habitat for Humanity building affordable housing for the poor and serves as an unofficial U.S. ambassador to the world's trouble spots. The **Jimmy Carter National Historic Site and Preservation District** includes most of Plains, which has fewer than 700 people. The visitors center in Plains Depot served as his campaign headquarters and now displays his memorabilia. *FYI:* Main St., Plains; (912) 824-3413. **The Carter Presidential Center and Library** sits on a 30-acre hilltop with a Japanese garden overlooking Atlanta. It chronicles his life with 27 million documents and a full scale replica of the Oval Office. *FYI:* One Coppenhill Ave., Atlanta; (404) 331-0296.

Museum of the Jimmy Carter Library, Atlanta

Atlanta Convention & Visitor's Bureau

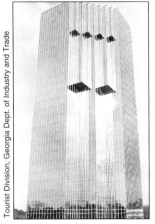

Tower Palace, an example of snazzy Atlanta architecture and a symbol of Georgia's growth

Tourist Division, Georgia Dept. of Industry and Trade

Georgia Grows

By 1990 Georgia's 6.6 million population made it the 11th most populous state. While the U.S. population grew 11.45 percent during the 1980s, Georgia's rose 19.1 percent. One out of every five persons was a new resident.

Events

Andersonville Historic Fair, May and October, offers Civil War reenactments, craftspeople, and 200 antique dealers. *FYI:* (912) 924-2558. **National Black Arts Festival** is a ten-day celebration in Metro Atlanta, with more than 150 programs celebrating African American artists.

THE NATURAL WORLD

In the Beginning

The entire record of geologic time is preserved in Georgia's rocks and land. Uplifting, water, and wind have shaped and refined the landscape. The state slopes southeast from the mountains to the sea and includes three basic geographical regions: the Appalachian Highlands, Piedmont, and the Coastal Plain.

Fossilized trilobites and corals from its mountains indicate that between 3 billion and 255 million years ago, Georgia, like much of North America, lay beneath an ancient ocean. About 580 million years ago, pressures inside the earth pushed land upward along with layers of rock, which were then condensed, buckled, and folded. Molten rock poured into cracks and flowed over the surface, then hardened and crystallized into granite, forming the base of the Appalachian Highlands and Piedmont Plateau.

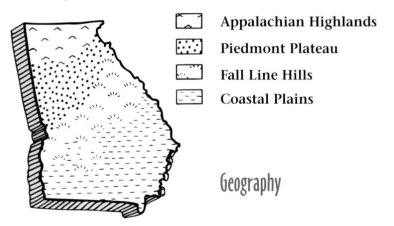

Appalachian Highlands

Piedmont Plateau

Fall Line Hills

Coastal Plains

Geography

Mountain Building

Through centuries, wind and rain worked their magic, eroding the highlands and depositing debris in the inland sea. Thousands of feet of sediment stacked up in layers. Eventually the land was lifted again, and the Appalachian Mountains began forming. The upheaval continued until about 300,000 years ago, when the area may have stood 10,000 feet higher than it does now.

While the Appalachian Mountains were forming, Georgia was tilted. Erosion increased, and most of the debris moved south to settle as the Piedmont's surface. Molten rock trapped beneath the bedrock eventually hardened and formed Stone Mountain. The Fall Line—an arc of low hills that extends from Augusta down through Macon and up to Columbus—marks the ancient beachline that separated the Piedmont from the sea.

Ancient Life

As millions of years passed, the Coastal Plain was created from materials carried to the ocean by wind and water. There it settled in layers of gravel, sand, and clay. Starting at the Fall Line hills, the land was laid down in successive layers, with the youngest at the coast.

Changes in land and climate brought a passing parade of prehistoric life to Georgia. Fossilized larch twigs and leaves at Dahlonega, and mastodon teeth found at Lithia Springs in northwestern Georgia date to 58 million years ago. Giant ground sloths roamed Skidaway Island, and the Brunswick and Savannah areas were stomping grounds for prehistoric megatheriums, mammoths, hippopotamuses, horses, oxen, and hogs. Some 63 million years ago, oysters up to 22 inches long lay in the sands near Augusta and central Georgia. About 40 million years ago, a toothed whale (now extinct) swam in the ocean near present-day Macon. Georgia's state fossil, the shark's tooth, has been found as far north as the Fall Line.

Georgia Southern University Museum: A 26-foot skeleton of a 78 million-year-old Mosasaur that swam the seas when dinosaurs ruled the earth is featured, along with changing exhibits and hands-on displays. Ten-acre GSU Botanical Gardens shows native plants, wildflowers, and wildlife. *FYI:* Statesboro; (912) 681-5444.

William Weinman Mineral Museum: The Southeast's only museum dedicated solely to rocks, minerals, and fossils exhibits gemstones, a man-made cave, and Indian artifacts. *FYI:* I-75 Exit 126, Cartersville; (404) 386-0576.

Fernbank Museum of Natural History: Fifteen galleries in the Southeast's largest natural history museum highlight dinosaurs, the origin of the universe, the Okefenokee Swamp, local seashells, and a 1,000-gallon living reef aquarium. "A Walk Through Time in Georgia" interprets the natural history of Georgia and the chronological development of the Earth. *FYI:* 767 Clifton Rd., N.E., Atlanta; (404) 378-0127.

Appalachian Highlands

North America's oldest mountain chain stretches from Georgia into Canada. The Appalachian's jumble of ridges and deep valleys fills approximately 2,000 square miles of northern Georgia.

The view from Lookout Mountain spreads across seven states

The region is a wonderland of scenic beauty punctuated by lakes, rivers, sharply serrated ridges, and a blaze of autumn colors. Some 747,000 acres of the **Chattahoochee National Forest**, with the nation's greatest diversity of trees, sprawls through the mountains and onto the Piedmont Plateau.

U.S. 76 meanders through the "Top of Georgia." Glassy lakes offer outdoor recreation—the rugged Chattooga River is famous for white water rafting. Many rivers begin in the Blue Ridge Mountains, Georgia's major watershed.

Numerous falls provide some of the most striking scenery. **Anna Ruby Falls** drops in a 150- and 50-foot-high double waterfall, 1.5 miles north of Unicoi State Park. *FYI:* (706) 878-2201. **De Soto Falls Scenic Area**, at a 2,000-3,400-foot elevation, provides several waterfalls within a three-mile radius. *FYI:* North of Dahlonega; (706) 864-3711. Two-mile-long **Tallulah Gorge** is believed to be the oldest natural chasm in North America. A trail along the rim of the 1,200-foot-deep canyon offers breathtaking views of three waterfalls, one of which plunges 700 feet to the gorge floor. *FYI:* U.S. 441; (706) 754-8257.

Russell-Brasstown Scenic Byway winds through the Bavarian theme village of Helen

Trekkin' and Travelin' the High Country

The **Appalachian Trail** begins in Georgia and concludes in Maine. It winds for 83 miles through the Chattahoochee National Forest and can be accessed from an eight-mile trail in **Amicalola Falls State Park**. At 729 feet Amicalola Falls is the highest waterfall east of the Rockies. The park offers cabins, campsites, and a restaurant. *FYI:* 16 miles northwest of Dawsonville; (706) 265-8888.

Russell-Brasstown Scenic Byway, a National Forest Service scenic byway, makes a 38-mile loop on Georgia Highways 12/75, 180, and 348 up to Brasstown Bald, across the Appalachian Trail, and by mountain streams. Elevations vary between 2,040 and 4,784 feet. **Brasstown Bald**, at 4,784 feet, is the state's highest point and offers views across Georgia into Tennessee, and North and South Carolina. *FYI:* (706) 896-2556. *FYI:* Chattahoochee National Forest, Gainesville; (404) 536-0541.

State Parks

Cloudland Canyon: Hang gliders launch from Lookout Mountain Flight Park. Rock City Gardens features 400 varieties of wildflowers and shrubs, and unique rock formations. *FYI:* 25 miles northwest of LaFayette on GA 136; (706) 657-4050.

Black Rock Mountain: Georgia's highest state park is situated astride the Eastern Continental Divide at a 3,640-foot elevation. A visitors center offers a spectacular 80-mile view of the southern Appalachians. *FYI:* Three miles north of Clayton; (706) 746-2141.

Moccasin Creek: Known as the park where "spring spends the summer," Moccasin Creek is nestled in mountains on the shores of Lake Burton. *FYI:* (706) 947-3194.

Georgia State Parks

Millions of years of geologic history are recorded in the rocks of Cloudland Canyon

The Piedmont

Piedmont means "foot of the mountain." It occupies about a third of Georgia between the Appalachian Highlands and the flat southern plains, and includes the major population centers of Atlanta, Columbus, and Macon. In the Piedmont elevations range from 400 feet along the southern fall line to 1,500 feet near the northern edge. It is a region of gently rolling red clay hills broken by ridges and deep river valleys.

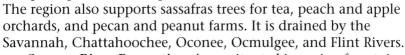

The **Oconee National Forest** covers 109,000 acres in two units between Athens and Macon. Hardwood trees are fewer here than in other parts; conifers like loblolly, short leaf, and pitch pine are more plentiful. The region also supports sassafras trees for tea, peach and apple orchards, and pecan and peanut farms. It is drained by the Savannah, Chattahoochee, Oconee, Ocmulgee, and Flint Rivers.

Oconee River Recreation Area, situated in a pine forest, is great for camping, canoeing, swimming, and boating. Lake Sinclair and the Ocmulgee River are famous for fishing. White-tailed deer, wild turkey, quail, and waterfowl congregate at the 27,000-acre Cedar Creek Game Management Area. **Piedmont National Wildlife Refuge** is a haven for the red-cockaded woodpecker and other endangered wildlife.

The Chattahoochee River extends from the mountainous northeast through the Piedmont's gently rolling hills. Many plants and trees common to both areas grow along its banks. Dogwoods, trout lilies, azaleas, asters, wild violets, cardinal flowers, and scarlet sumac light up heavily wooded forests and scenic rock outcroppings along the 48 miles of the **Chattahoochee River National Recreation Area**. The usually slow-moving river is a favorite of rafters, who may spot fox and raccoons in the hardwood forests, and beaver, muskrats and turtles along river banks. *FYI:* Chattahoochee National Recreation Area; (404) 399-8070. The **Chattahoochee Nature Center** offers a bird of prey rehabilitation program and a boardwalk for observing wildlife and the river marsh. *FYI:* 9135 Willeo Rd., Roswell; (404) 992-2055.

At the Fall Line, rivers tumble from the Piedmont plateau and cascade onto the Coastal Plain lowlands. Huge granite outcroppings mark the Fall Line at **Old Clinton Roadside Park**. *FYI:* U.S. 129.

Stone Mountain

The Piedmont's most prominent natural landmark is also the world's largest exposed granite monolith. It stands 825 feet high, rises 1,683 feet above sea level, and covers 583 acres. The rock was formed approximately 300 million years ago, when molten lava trapped beneath the surface hardened into a two-mile-thick layer. It was exposed as the earth's cover eroded during the next 200 million years. Stone Mountain is unique in that its chemical composition and physical characteristics differ from all other stone in the Southeast. The famous bas-relief sculpture of Confederate President Jefferson Davis, Robert E. Lee, and Stonewall Jackson adorns its north face. Visitors can hike or ride a tram to the summit. *FYI:* 16 miles east of Atlanta on GA 78; (404) 498-5690.

At **Panola Mountain State Conservation Park**, a granite dome monadnock covers 100 acres, offering hiking trails and wildlife specific to the Piedmont region. *FYI:* 2600 Hwy. 155, S.W., Stockbridge; (404) 389-7801.

Atlanta Convention and Visitor's Bureau

Although Stone Mountain dominates the countryside, it is only the tip of a rock formation which lies beneath the Piedmont

Georgia State Parks

Wind and rain have worked their magic to create colorful ridges and spires at Providence Canyon

Coastal Plain

The ocean's slow withdrawal left an extensive coastal plain that covers the entire southern half of the state. It drops only 500 feet in the 150 miles from the Fall Line to the coast and hundreds of offshore islands, some of which form a natural barrier protecting the shoreline from storms and high waters.

Providence Canyon

Often called "Georgia's Little Grand Canyon," this chasm's cliffs, spires, and serrated ridges are streaked with bands of orange, yellow, purples, greys, and various shades of scarlet. The rare plumleaf azalea, which blooms in July and August, grows only in this area. *FYI:* Seven miles west of Lumpkin; (912) 838-6202.

Okefenokee Swamp

Okefenokee, an Anglo translation of an Indian word, means "trembling earth." Extending 38 miles north to south, and 25 miles east to west, it is the second largest freshwater swamp in the United States. Numerous islands, lakes, and prairies separate moss-covered cypress, blackgum, and bay forests.

Masses of decaying plant material covered with bushes and weeds float on dark brown water, which is colored by tannic acid released from decaying vegetation. The swamp is a habitat for 621 species of plants, 39 species of fish, 37 types of amphibians, 64 reptile varieties, 235 different birds, and 50 mammal species. Among the animals are the

Georgia State Parks

Stephen C. Foster State Park borders Okefenokee Swamp and is a habitat for American alligators

endangered red-cockaded woodpecker, wood stork, and American bald eagle. Visitors centers offer interpretive programs and walking trails. *FYI:* East entrance: Suwannee Canal Recreation Area. North entrance: Okefenokee Swamp Park; (912) 283-0583. West entrance: Stephen C. Foster State Park; (912) 637-5274.

The Golden Isles

Georgia's Atlantic coastline stretches 100 miles south from the Savannah River to the St. Marys River. The total distance around the bays, river mouths, and coastal islands is 2,344 miles.

From the 1880s to the 1940s, the Golden Isles were vacation spots for America's wealthiest industrialists. The eight islands off the Brunswick coast are Ossabaw, Wassaw, St. Catherines, St. Simons, Jekyll, Sea, Sapelo, and Cumberland. Wildlife watchers may be rewarded with sightings of great blue herons, white egrets, porpoises, pelicans, deer, armadillos, fiddler crabs, and offshore manatees. The knobbed whelk, Georgia's official state seashell, is found in coastal waters. *FYI:* Brunswick and the Golden Isles Visitors Bureau, (912) 265-0622; outside Georgia, (800) 933-COAST.

Brunswick & Golden Isles Visitors Bureau

The Golden Isles were the place to see and be seen at the turn of the century

Marshes of Glynn

In 1878 Georgia poet Sidney Lanier immortalized these wetlands in "The Marshes of Glynn" while sitting under an oak on the Brunswick mainland. Lanier Oak still stands in **Marshes of Glynn Overlook Park**, which provides a good view of the offshore marshes. They are considered some of the world's most pro-

ductive wetlands. A habitat for birds, shrimp, crab, and oyster larvae, they figure in the life cycle of more than 70 percent of the fish and provide essential support for Georgia's seafood industry.

Cumberland Island National Seashore

Cumberland Island, the southernmost and largest of Georgia's barrier islands, contains the ruins of the Carnegie family estate, as well as colorful birds, wild horses, and nesting loggerhead turtles. *FYI:* National Park Service, St. Marys, (912) 882-4336; (912) 882-4335 for tour reservations.

Rivers

Approximately half of Georgia's 17 major rivers and many streams flow south and east into the Atlantic Ocean. In western Georgia they empty into the Gulf of Mexico, either by flowing south, or north by way of the Ohio, Tennessee, and Mississippi Rivers. The longest are the 350-mile Savannah and the 330-mile Chattahoochee. The Chattooga River's striking scenery and thrilling rapids are protected under the National Wild and Scenic Rivers Act. Other major rivers include the Alapaha, Altamaha, Canoochee, Flint, Ochlockonee, Ocmulgee, Oconee, Ohoopee, Satilla, and Withlacoochee.

Harnessing the Resources

Although natural lakes can be found throughout Georgia, the largest are reservoirs, which have been created by damming rivers to provide irrigation, flood control, and hydroelectric power.

1) Allatoona Lake, on the Appalachian Highlands' Etowah River, has more than 12,000 acres of water surface and 270 miles of shoreline. The project started in 1941, was interrupted by World War II, and began operations in 1950. The lake depth sometimes fluctuates by three to four feet daily; during heavy rains, it may rise up to 20 feet in a week's time. Facilities include 36 public use

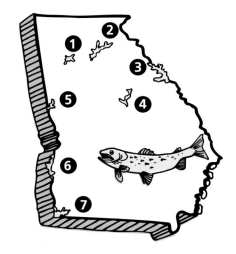

Georgia's Lakes

areas, multiple boat launches, marinas, and swimming beaches. *FYI:* (404) 386-0549. **Red Top Mountain State Park** and lodge are located on a 1,950-acre peninsula of Lake Allatoona. *FYI:* 653 Red Top Mountain Rd., S.E., Cartersville; (404) 975-0055.

2) **Lake Sidney Lanier**'s multiple arms extend through the northern mountains; they were formed by damming the Chattahoochee. Several peaks remained above water and became islands. Resort facilities range from children's playgrounds to championship golf courses. *FYI:* 6950 Holiday Rd., Buford; (404) 932-7200.

3) **J. Strom Thurmond Lake**, with 1,200 miles of shoreline, borders South Carolina. The 38-mile-long reservoir on the Savannah River is the largest Corps of Engineers project east of the Mississippi. More than 7 million people use it each year for water-based recreation. Wildlife management programs have made it a prime area for duck, deer, and turkey hunting, as well as wildlife watching. *FYI:* 22 miles north of Augusta; (404) 722-3770.

4) **Lake Oconee and Lake Sinclair** are fed by the Oconee River. Set in the rolling hills and forests of the eastern Piedmont, they provide about 34,000 acres of water and 800 miles of shoreline. Record-breaking bass and other fishing tournaments are held on them. *FYI:* Georgia Power Company, 239 Lawrence Shoals Rd., N.E., Eatonton; (404) 485-8704.

5) **West Point Lake**'s multiple arms reach into Alabama and the Piedmont. More than 500 miles of shoreline with extensive public use areas surround 25,900 acres of Chattahoochee water. *FYI:* Four miles north of West Point; (706) 645-2929.

6) **Walter F. George** is one of two major lakes in the southwest coastal plain. The 48,000-acre Corps of Engineers project has 643 miles of shoreline and the second highest lock east of the Mississippi. **Florence Marina State Park** on the Chattahoochee River offers multiple opportunities for water sports. *FYI:* (912) 838-4244.

7) **Lake Seminole**, situated at the confluence of the Chattahoochee and Flint Rivers, fills 47 miles of deep channels. It is one of the nation's prime bass lakes. *FYI:* 16 miles south of Donalsonville on GA 39; (912) 861-3137.

Digging Georgia

Georgia's good earth has found a ready market since 1766, when its clay was shipped to England's famous Wedgwood pottery factory. Prior to 1849 Georgia led the United States in gold mining. Georgia granite, limestone, and clay have been used in brick since the 1880s. More than 100,000 tons of coal were mined in 1881, and the nation's first bauxite was discovered near Rome in 1887. In the 1930s, Georgia was a leading producer of Fuller's earth, manganese, and barite.

Dahlonega is the site of America's first gold rush, which lasted more than 20 years

The U.S. Capitol contains Georgia granite and its abundant marble is used extensively in buildings and monuments. Kaolin, a chalky white clay, is Georgia's largest export, and is used to make white ware, firebrick, terra cotta, paint, and fine china. The state also produces much of the world's talc and soapstone, and is an important supplier of feldspar, mica, and limestone. **Elberton Granite Museum** relates the town's rise to "Granite Capital of the World" with films and exhibits. *FYI:* GA 17 & 712, Granite; (706) 283-5651.

Forests and Flowers

Forests cover more than two-thirds of Georgia. While some of the main trees are oaks, hickories, and cypresses, the state is famous for its pines, which include shortleaf and loblolly. Gums from longleaf and slash pines are refined into turpentine, resin, tar, and pitch.

Magnolias are part of the romantic literature of the South. The colorful bouquet of wildflowers includes the Confederate rose and daisy, red sumac, crimson trumpet vine, Queen Anne's lace, rhododendron, flame azalea, and the state flower, the Cherokee rose. Some mountain plants, such as wild columbine, Dutchman's breeches, and lily of the valley, are usually found only in New England and Eastern Canada.

Wildlife

Along with 350 species of birds, Georgia is home to several unusual animals and species. The anhinga of Okefenokee Swamp is also called the "water turkey." It uses its wings to swim under water while catching fish. Manatees, sometimes called "sea cows," are found offshore. They can weigh up to 3,500 pounds and belong to an order of mammals more closely related to elephants than to whales or seals.

Loggerhead turtles grow to 43 inches long and 880 pounds. Females come ashore only at night to lay eggs, then immediately return to the sea. Black right whales, one of the world's rarest species, live within five to ten miles of the coast. Beware of alligators and the poisonous rattlesnake, copperhead, water moccasin (cottonmouth), and coral snake.

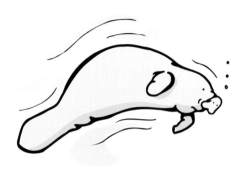

The shy manatee is also known as a "sea cow"

Weathering the Weather

Generally, Georgia enjoys a mild climate. Although it receives an average yearly rainfall of 50 inches, less than 1.5 inches fall as snow. Summer temperatures average between 73 and 82 degrees Fahrenheit, while winters usually fall between 41 and 56 degrees. Unseasonably warm days often occur during winter. January temperatures of 80 degrees have been recorded as far north as Rome. Tornadoes are threats in the mountains, and hurricanes occur near the coast.

Temperature Trivia

Georgia's hottest recorded temperature was 113° F at Greenville, on May 27, 1978. The coldest temperature of -17° F was recorded on January 27, 1940, in northwest Georgia.

GOING TO TOWN

Atlanta

Pop.: 394,017
Elev.: 940–1,050 ft.
Noted for: Host city, 1996 Olympics; Atlanta Cyclorama; CNN Cable Broadcasting; Martin Luther King Jr. Historic District; Six Flags Over Georgia; Zoo Atlanta; Underground Atlanta; World of Coca-Cola; Atlanta Braves baseball; Atlanta Falcons NFL football; Atlanta Hawks NBA basketball.
Nearby: Stone Mountain; Kennesaw Mountain National Battlefield; Allatoona Lake; Panola Mountain Conservation Park; Chattahoochee River National Recreation Area.
Visitors Information: (404) 521-6600

Georgia's state capitol, built in 1889, is topped by a gold dome. Inside, visit the Hall of Fame and the State Museum of Science and Industry.

Founded in 1837 as the southern terminus of the Western and Atlantic Railroad, Atlanta became a major transportation hub, manufacturing center, and supply depot. After Sherman's army burned it to the ground in 1864, it rebounded to become the capital in 1868 and has enjoyed steady growth ever since. In 1963 it took the lead in the civil rights movement when its mayor was the only southern mayor to testify before Congress in support of the pending Civil Rights Bill.

Approximately 37 percent of Georgia residents live in the greater Atlanta area. As the county seat, state capital, and regional headquarters for federal government, it has the largest concentration of federal and regional offices outside Washington, D.C. Atlanta has become one of the world's largest air transportation centers and one of North America's premier convention and tourist destinations. Facilities include the world's largest airport terminal and the tallest hotel in the Western Hemisphere. You'll need a map to find your way around, as more than 40 streets contain the name *Peachtree*.

Events
April: Atlanta Dogwood Festival
July: Annual African American Street Festival

Progressive Government

About half of the private property in Georgia was destroyed during the American Revolution. To encourage settlement the state government awarded free land grants of up to 1,000 acres to war veterans and their families. After the Revolution Georgia created a constitution that allowed more people to vote and take part in government than in most of the other new states.

Georgia Dept. of Industry and Trade

The Old Governor's Mansion reflects the elegance of Milledgeville. It was one of the few cities that was planned as a seat of state government.

Marietta (pop. 44,100, elev. 1,118 ft.): The Cobb County Seat was founded in 1834. By the early 1800s it was a bustling commercial center and resort that attracted coastal residents seeking to escape the summer's heat. After Sherman's destruction, recovery was slow. Marietta is one of the few towns with both a Union and Confederate cemetery. **Noted for:** Lockheed Aircraft, the state's largest employer; four National Register Historic Districts with more than 150 antebellum and Victorian homes. *FYI:* (404) 429-1115.

Decatur (pop. 17,300): Most of the Battle of Atlanta was fought in Decatur, and much of the town was completely destroyed by fire. The DeKalb County Seat is home to several high tech companies, the National Centers for Disease Control and Prevention, and the American Cancer Society national headquarters. Decatur will host five Olympic events. **Noted for:** Fernbank Science Center; Chamblee's Antique Row; DeKalb Farmers Market; Soapstone Center for the Arts. *FYI:* (404) 378-2525; outside Georgia, (800) 999-6055.

Fitzgerald was originally settled by retired Union veterans. Its streets are named for Union and Confederate generals. The town's prime attraction is the Blue and Gray Museum. *FYI:* Municipal Building, Old Depot; (912) 423-5375.

Columbus

Pop.: 179,300
Elev.: 261 feet
Noted for: Fountains; Columbus Riverwalk; Columbus Ironworks; historic district; Pemberton House; Springer Opera House; National Infantry Museum; Confederate Naval Museum.
Nearby: Pine Mountain Wild Animal Park; Warm Springs and Little White House; Callaway Gardens; Providence Canyon.
Visitors Information: (706) 322-1613; outside Georgia, (800) 999-1613

Columbus' Illges House, built in the 1850s, is considered one of America's finest examples of Greek Revival architecture

Tourism Division, Georgia Dept. of Industry and Trade

Founded by a state legislative act in 1827, Columbus began as a Chattahoochee River port. By 1850 the town of fewer than 6,000 people had attracted Irish, Scottish, English, German, French, Danish, Swiss, and Italian settlers.

During the Civil War it was a major production center for cloth, Colt Navy pistols, cannons, rifles, and swords. The Confederate Naval Ironworks and Shipyards manufactured engines and machinery. General James Winslow, unaware that Lee had surrendered, burned the town, including its factories, supplies, and depot, on April 17, 1863.

Fort Benning was established during World War I and boosted the economy through the Depression and World War II. Many textile companies are located in Columbus, along with Royal Crown Cola and AT&T Universal Card Services Corporation. A major port, it is the northernmost navigable point on the Chattahoochee River and Georgia's western border. The Riverfront Industrial District is a National Historic Landmark.

Bad River

It took more than ten years to make the Chattahoochee River navigable downstream from Columbus. Out of 43 vessels operating on the river before 1853, 20 were wrecked or burned due to shallow water, snags, fire, and boiler explosions.

Events

April: Riverfest Weekend
September: Southern Open PGA Golf Tournament
November: Columbus Steeplechase

Savannah

Pop.: 137,560
Elev.: 43 feet
Noted for: Nation's largest registered historic district; Savannah History Museum; Juliette Gordon Low Birthplace; Ships of the Sea Museum; Telfair Academy of Arts and Sciences; historic churches; Beach Institute.
Nearby: Fort Pulaski National Monument; Tybee Island Lighthouse; Savannah National Wildlife Refuge.
Visitors Information: (800) 444-2427

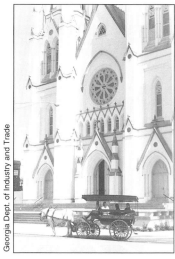

Georgia Dept. of Industry and Trade

Classical architecture and horse-drawn carriages contribute to the charm of Savannah

Georgia's "Mother City" was designed by founder James Oglethorpe from sketches drawn by Robert Castell. Although Castell's blueprints emphasized freedom and space, he died in an English debtor's prison. During the American Revolution, some 2,000 British troops seized the town, which was defended by 600 rebels who had harassed the Royal Governor and driven him back to England. Afterwards it prospered as the leading shipping port for cotton, naval stores, and tobacco. In 1819 history was made when the *City of Savannah* sailed from the harbor and became the first steamboat to cross the Atlantic. Sherman ended his march to the sea at Savannah, and it remained in Union hands until war's end.

A major manufacturing center, Savannah is the largest foreign commerce port on the south Atlantic coast and the regional hub for approximately 20 Georgia and South Carolina counties. Often called one of America's most beautiful cities, Savannah contains many 19th-century homes renowned for their refinement and ornate iron work.

Savannah Firsts
1733–America's first planned city, Georgia's first city and first capital; 1735–First silk exportation from America; 1736–First American Sunday School; 1794–America's first golf course.

Events
February: Georgia Heritage Celebration
August: Savannah Maritime Festival

Macon

Pop.: 118,420
Elev.: 335 feet
Noted for: Sidney Lanier Cottage; Hay House; Old Cannonball House and Confederate Museum; historic districts; Harriet Tubman Historical & Cultural Museum; Museum of Arts and Sciences; Rose Hill Cemetery; Wesleyan College.

Georgia Dept. of Industry and Trade

The Hay House is a Macon monument to the Victorian era

Nearby: Ocmulgee National Monument; Lake Tobesofkee Recreation Area; Lake Juliette; Piedmont National Wildlife Refuge; Georgia Agricenter.
Visitors Information: (912) 743-3401

When President Thomas Jefferson ordered the establishment of Fort Benjamin Hawkins in 1806, the area became Georgia's western frontier. Macon was platted in 1822, with stipulations that it contain wide streets and that all lot owners plant shade trees on their properties. With its cotton-based economy and Fall Line site, Macon bustled with boat, stage coach, and train traffic. By 1822 it was the Bibb County Seat. The *Macon Telegraph* newspaper, which is still published, was established in 1826, as was the Georgia Female College. Now Wesleyan College, it was the first college chartered specifically to grant degrees to women. During the Civil War Macon withstood three Union attacks. Its Confederate depository held $1.5 million in gold, while its factories produced cannons, harnesses, shot, and small arms. The Old Cannonball House and Confederate Museum was the only building to sustain damage. When Sherman took Milledgeville, the state capital was relocated to Macon. It continues to be an important economic, cultural, educational, and medical center. The Japanese Counsel General named it the "Cherry Blossom Capital of the World." With 350 churches, it claims more churches per capita than any other city in the nation.

Events

March: Cherry Blossom Festival
September: Southern Jubilee
October: Arrowhead Arts & Crafts Festival

Albany

Pop.: 110,435
Elev.: 210 feet
Noted for: Albany Museum of Art; Thronateeska Heritage Center; Wetherbee Planetarium; Miniature Train Exhibit; Fall on the Flint Festival in September.
Nearby: Chehaw Wild Animal Park; Radium Springs; Fossil Sand Dunes; hunting preserves; Lake Blackshear; Georgia Agrirama; Jimmy Carter National Historic Site.
Visitors Information: (912) 434-8700

In 1836 Alexander Shotwell, a New Jersey Quaker, bought land and hired surveyors to plat a town. During the same year, Colonel Nelson Tift sailed up the Flint River and began constructing the first log buildings. Indians were displaced, and settlement followed. Named after Albany, New York, it was chartered by the legislature in 1841. When John Fort drilled Georgia's first artesian well in 1841, he hit water at 450 feet and solved an area health problem created by contaminated surface streams. Albany was a Confederate meat packing center, and later became a commercial packing center for processing cattle, hogs, and sheep, lard, hides, wood, and sheepskins. After

When in Albany, consider a day-trip to the Georgia Agrirama, in nearby Tifton

decades of growing cotton, Albany farmers switched to pecans. Radium Springs, the semitropical climate, and nearby sand dunes have made Albany a popular stopover for golfers, swimmers, and sun worshippers. The Dougherty County Seat is southwest Georgia's largest city and the birthplace of Ray Charles.

Fossil Dunes
Remnants of ancient sand dunes, which some geologists believe were part of the northern edge of the Gulf of Mexico about a million years ago, extend along the Flint River and reach their peak near Albany.

Near the University of Georgia campus, College Square is a happenin' place

Athens

Pop.: 45,700
Elev.: 800 feet
Noted for: University of Georgia; U.S. Navy Supply Corps Museum; Taylor-Grady House; Tree That Owns Itself; Double-Barreled Cannon; Georgia Museum of Art; Founder's Memorial Gardens; State Botanical Garden of Georgia; home of R.E.M., B-52's.
Nearby: Watson Mill Bridge State Park; Oconee National Forest; Hard Labor Creek State Park.
Visitors Information: (706) 546-1805

The largest city in the northeastern Piedmont was named after Athens, Greece, the classical center of learning. It grew up around the University of Georgia, which was founded in 1875 as America's first state-chartered college. During the first 16 years the university existed only on paper. The first classes were held in 1801, and the town was incorporated five years later. It soon became the cultural center of Georgia. So many of its students enlisted in the Civil War that the university was forced to close and its buildings were converted into hospitals and barracks. After the war, it reopened, and the university is today the town's largest employer. It is ranked among the nation's top research institutions and is home of the Peabody Awards for broadcasting excellence. Twenty-three Georgia governors have graduated from the the University of Georgia.

Athens also is the shopping and service center for northeast Georgia. Its more than 100 manufacturers and processors include the oldest textile mill in operation south of the Potomac. The town also had one of the state's first paper mills and brick works. In 1891 the nation's first formal Ladies' Garden Club, with a constitution, by-laws, offices, and strict parliamentary laws, was organized here.

Events
April/May: Athens New Jazz Festival
October: Golden Gingko Festival

Augusta

Pop.: 44,600
Elev.: 162 feet
Noted for: Masters Golf Tournament; historic districts and churches; Confederate Powder Works; Cotton Exchange; Morris Museum of Art; National Science Center.
Nearby: J. Strom Thurmond Lake; Mistletoe State Park; Fort Gordon Military Reservation; Elijah Clark Memorial State Park.
Visitor's Information: (706) 724-4067; outside Georgia, (800) 726-0243

In 1735 James Oglethorpe established Augusta as a trading and military post. He named it after King George's mother. When the British took Savannah during the American Revolution, the colonial governor and his council fled to Augusta, and it remained the capital until 1796. Beginning in 1780, the town shifted back and forth between British and American control, finally falling to the English. "Lighthorse Harry" Lee recaptured it in 1781. After the war, Augusta became Georgia's major cotton and tobacco markets. With more than 200 brokers buying and selling around the globe at the Cotton Exchange, it was the world's second largest cotton market.

Augusta escaped destruction because Sherman lacked the resources to mount a siege. Because it offered highway, rail, and river transportation, the Confederate Powder Works were located in Augusta and during three years of operations produced more than 2 million pounds of gun powder. The factory's 176-foot chimney is the only remaining structure commissioned by the Confederacy.

Augusta shares its metropolitan population with South Carolina. The city contains hundreds of historic homes and a Riverfront Esplanade with several parks. It is a manufacturing center for fabrics, sportswear, chemicals, thermal ceramics, and utility vehicles.

Events
January: Augusta Cutting Horse Futurity Festival
March: Regattafest
April: Masters Golf Tournament

Valdosta

Pop.: 41,575
Elev.: 215 feet
Noted for: Historic district; shopping; The Crescent Complex; Lowndes County Historical Society Museum; Valdosta State College; Valdosta Aloft Arts Festival in April.
Nearby: Grand Bay Wildlife Management Area; Banks Lake National Wildlife Refuge; Okefenokee Swamp; Reed Bingham State Park; Florida border.
Visitors Information: (912) 245-0513

In 1860 Troupville's townspeople heard that the railroad line between Savannah and Mobile, Alabama, would bypass their community. So they packed up everything, including the county seat, and moved four miles southeast to the tracks. To honor a former Georgia governor, they named the new town after his estate, Val De Aosta. Prosperity came in the form of railroads, rich farmland, cotton, and pine forests, which were tapped for lumber, pulpwood, and turpentine. By 1910 *Fortune* magazine had named it America's richest city in per capita income. After boll weevils devastated cotton crops in 1917, farmers turned to growing tobacco. Situated eight miles north of the Florida line on Interstate 75, Valdosta's accessibility makes it attractive to a variety of industries. Seven Fortune 500 companies and several French and German firms are located in Lowndes County.

Infamous Son

John Henry "Doc" Holliday, son of Valdosta's mayor, practiced dentistry in that town. Troubled by tuberculosis, he moved to Arizona and earned a reputation as a gambler and gunfighter. Doc Holliday's most famous altercation came when he sided with Wyatt Earp in the legendary gunfight at the OK Corral. Unlike many gunfighters who died with their boots on, Holliday passed away peacefully in bed.

Rome

Pop.: 30,300
Elev.: 603 feet
Noted for: Chieftains Museum; Berry College; Oak Hill; Myrtle Hill Cemetery; nine national historic districts; Old Town Clock Tower; Coosa Valley Arts and Crafts Fair over Memorial Day Weekend; October Heritage Holidays.
Nearby: Cave Spring; James H. Floyd State Park; Etowah Mounds; Allatoona Lake.
Visitors Information: (706) 295-5576

Rome's Capitoline Wolf *is a reproduction of the original Etruscan piece and was given to the city in 1929 by Benito Mussolini*

Greater Rome Convention & Visitors Bureau

Founded in 1834 the town, like its namesake, was built on seven hills. As rowdy land speculators, outlaws, and vigilante committees gave way to cotton mills, tanneries, and iron works, Rome became northwest Georgia's leading industrial city. Sherman directed part of his Atlanta campaign from Rome before destroying its mills and factories. In 1902 Martha Berry founded Berry College. With aid from Henry Ford and other philanthropists, the school grew to 26,000 acres and became the world's largest college campus. Rome's Old Town Clock is on the National Register of Historic Places and has been a local landmark since 1872.

John Wisdom's Ride

In 1863, after mail carrier John Wisdom heard the Union army was

heading toward Rome, he took off on one of history's greatest rides. Discarding his buggy after 22 miles, he changed horses five times and galloped 67 miles in less than 8½ hours to warn the citizenry. Approaching Yankees saw Rome's defenders armed with squirrel rifles, shotguns, and muzzle-loading muskets. They retreated and were captured by Confederate general Nathan Bedford Forrest. Wisdom estimated he lost about an hour and a half begging and borrowing horses. One was lame and another threw him. Rome rewarded him with $400 in cash and a $400 silver service, which he treasured.

Gainesville

Pop.: 17,900
Elev.: 1,227 feet
Noted for: Lake Sidney Lanier; chicken and egg capital of the world; Georgia Mountain Museum; NASCAR Winston Racing Series and the Mule Camp Market, both in October.
Nearby: Dahlonega; Blue Ridge Mountains; De Soto Falls.
Visitors Information: (404) 536-5209

Tourist Division, Ga. Dept. of Industry and Trade

Road Atlanta, a premier racing facility for cars, motorcycles, and go-karts, is one of Gainesville's most popular attractions

The largest city in northeast Georgia and the Hall County Seat, Gainesville is surrounded by the Chattahoochee River arm of Lake Sidney Lanier. It is the heart of Georgia's chicken and egg industry and a major service area for outdoor recreation. Incorporated in 1821, the town's name honors General Edmund P. Gaines, known for arresting Aaron Burr and serving in the War of 1812 and the Black Hawk and Seminole Wars. Until the construction of the Charlotte and Atlanta Railroad, Gaineville's main attraction was its proximity to the Dahlonega gold fields. The chicken and egg business began in the 1890s, when mountain farmers began bringing poultry products to town and created a major market. By 1899 it was the first town south of Baltimore with electrically lighted streets. A 1936 tornado leveled 992 buildings, injured 950 people, and took 170 lives as it cut an eight-mile by one-mile swath through the town.

General James Longstreet

Confederate General James Longstreet, affectionately referred to by General Robert E. Lee as "my old war horse," lived in Gainesville from 1875 until his death in 1904. He operated the Piedmont Hotel and made it his base during his long political career as a Republican party leader. He also owned a 45-acre farm and was very proud of the wine from his vineyard. Portions of the hotel, including a room where Woodrow Wilson stayed, still stand. The general and his family are buried in Gainesville's Alta Vista Cemetery.

Waycross (pop. 20,000, elev. 135 feet) has been a crossroads for Indian, pioneer, and military trails; stage coach routes; and railroads. Its name was shortened from "the place where the ways cross." Founded in 1872 it is the largest city in Georgia's largest county and the economic center for an eight-county region. Former residents include actors Burt Reynolds, Pernell Roberts, and Ossie Davis; and music's Gram Parsons. **Noted for:** Okefenokee Swamp; Obediah's Okefenok; Laura S. Walker State Park. *FYI:* (912) 283-3742.

Brunswick (pop. 17,256, elev. 14 feet) is the gateway to the Golden Isles and the base for Georgia's commercial shrimp and seafood fleet. Established by the Royal Province of Georgia in 1771, it was named for the German ancestral home of King George II. By the 1900s Brunswick ranked first among Georgia cities in exporting lumber, second in naval stores, and third in cotton. Tourism, the

Brunswick and the Golden Isles Visitors Bureau

Brunswick's shrimp boat fleet is a major contributor to the local economy and a favorite visitor attraction

Georgia Pacific Corporation, seafood processing, and tool manufacturing now comprise its major industries. **Noted for:** Shrimp docks; Lover's Oak; Old Town National Register District; Lanier Oak and Overlook Park; Hofwyl-Broadfield Plantation. *FYI:* (912) 265-0620; outside Georgia, (800) 933-COAST.

Pogo's Place

Waycross and Okefenokee Swamp are the home of Pogo, the cartoon opossum. Cartoonist Walt Kelly created the comic strip in the late 1940s as a political satire that highlighted environmental problems. Kelly placed Pogo, Albert alligator, Bearegard hound dog, and other creatures in Okefenokee Swamp, because it was a natural habitat basically unspoiled by man. Twenty years after Kelly's death, the strip still appears in more than 200 newspapers. **Okefenokee Heritage Center** in Waycross contains the world's only Walt Kelly Room. *FYI:* (912) 285-4260.

TASTE OF GEORGIA

Down-Home Cooking

Although there are no hard-and-fast rules about Southern cooking, when you sit down at the table, you know your meal is going to be diverse and incredibly satisfying. While some of the best Southern cooks don't put recipes in writing, they know precisely how much of each ingredient to use. Although some doubt that there is a distinctive Georgia cuisine, just about everyone agrees that certain dishes are associated with Southern cooking.

You know you're talking Southern cooking when the pungent aromas of catfish and collards, fried chicken with cream gravy, or grits and ham fill the air. Or when you settle down to pork chops and sweet potato casserole, and dip into side dishes of butter beans and baked summer squash. With those basics you can cook anything from a simple meal to an elaborate feast.

One Pot Dishes

One pot dishes, a mixture of seafood, meat, and vegetables, start with a variety of spices and vegetables, including sliced celery, onion, potatoes, and several ears of corn. Throw in some fresh sausage or beef, shrimp or oysters, let it cook, and you've got a meal that's been a favorite for generations.

Low Country Cooking

Along the Georgia and South Carolina coasts, Low Country cooking has been a tradition since colonial days. Coastal tide flats have provided ideal conditions for the main ingredient, rice. Tomatoes, corn, and hominy (hulled and dried corn kernels with bran and germ removed) became part of the stew. West Indies traders brought hot and spicy peppers, cayenne, mustard, and pepper sherry. African slaves contributed okra seeds, which they sowed on plantations and wore as talismans.

Crabs, clams, oysters, and shrimp are abundant and important ingredients in Low Country cooking. Deer, duck, marsh hens, and quail round out the list. If you travel along the Georgia coast, you'll find a variety of Low Country cooking in time-honored dishes like catfish, deviled crab, fried shrimp, and jambalaya.

Cornucopia

The state's cuisine has been influenced by everyone from Georgia farmers to English noblemen. You can eat your way through Georgia on barbecue alone. Barbecuing is more than a tradition; it's an obsession that comes complete with festivals and cook-offs. Just about everyone will tell you that barbecue made in one area tastes completely  different from that concocted anywhere else. There are also endless recipes and entrees celebrating peaches, peanuts, pecans, and poultry. Sophisticated gourmet dining with American, continental, Oriental, and other flairs are common in many Georgia cities.

Bad Water, Good Whiskey

While Georgia's swamps and tide flats yielded an abundance of food, much of the water was not fit for consumption. In colonial times, alcohol proved a viable substitute. Beer, brandy, rum, whiskey, and wine were readily available and kept many drunk all the time. It was not unusual for children to drink beer and alcoholic cider, and for adults to consume approximately half a pint of rum per day.

Farming the Land

Georgia's colonists stepped off the boat hoping to raise rice, plant vineyards, and establish a silk industry. Everyone, including doctors, lawyers, merchants, and teachers, initially farmed. Although the silk and wine industries failed, by 1752 the 2,000 Anglos living in Georgia were harvesting rice, wheat, corn, peas, and indigo. Once cotton became king, it continued as the dominant industry into the 20th century. After boll weevils devastated cotton crops in the 1920s, many farmers turned to growing fruits and nuts.

Peaches, Georgia's most famous commodity, ripen from June through August

Tourist Division, Ga. Dept. of Industry and Trade

The Peach State

In 1875 Samuel Henry Rumph developed a new peach and named it the Elberta in honor of his wife. By 1919 there were 12 million peach trees growing in the Piedmont alone. Georgia called itself "the Peach State," and even named a county after the luscious fruit.

Fragrant pink and white peach blossoms blanket the landscape during the last two weeks in March. The state-designated **Peach Blossom Trail** (U.S. 341 west of I-75) stretches from Jonesboro to Perry, and meanders for 100 miles through eight counties that grow 65 percent of Georgia's peaches. En route you can visit packing sheds and buy peaches fresh from roadside stands. *FYI:* Call (404) 968-8990 for a *Peach Blossom Trail Guide*.

Crop Capitals

Southern Georgia is the world's pecan capital and produces one-third of the pecans on the American market. In 1931 Toombs County farmer Mose Coleman discovered his onions were sweet and could be eaten raw, like apples. The sensational taste of vidalia onions created a $30 million industry for 20 counties. Brunswick boasts of being the world's shrimp capital, while Cordele makes a similar claim for watermelons. Ellijay designated itself Georgia's apple capital, and Alma elevated itself to capital status by producing more than six million pounds of blueberries annually.

Peanut Trivia
A peanut is not a nut. It's a legume that grows close to the ground, flowers above the surface, then penetrates the soil, where it matures. Peanuts may have originated in Brazil. Traders and explorers took them to Asia and Africa, from which slaves brought them to America. **George Washington Carver** developed more than 300 uses for peanuts, and once created a nine-course meal in which every dish—from salad to coffee—was made with them. They are also used in cosmetics, dyes, axle grease, paints, plastics, linoleum, and explosives.

Peanuts are the world's most popular "nut" and one of the top ten cash crops nationally and internationally

Peanut Advisory Board

Peanuts

Until the Civil War, when starving soldiers began gobbling them up, the lowly peanut was raised primarily as food for slaves and cattle. Georgia, with more than 600,000 acres of peanuts, leads the nation in peanut production, growing 1.5 to 2 billion pounds each year. All those peanuts pump about $2.5 billion into the state's economy.

Poultry
Georgia is the leading producer of chickens and eggs. Every day its poultry farms produce and process more than 6.7 million pounds of chickens and sell 12 million eggs. The center of poultry production is Gainesville.

Favorite Recipes

Chatham Artillery Punch

The Chatham Artillery was organized May 1, 1786, and is Georgia's oldest military organization. Its first official duty was at General Nathanael Greene's funeral. The artillery saluted George Washington on his 1791 visit to Savannah with 26 firings of their field pieces. Washington liked them so much that he gave them the "Washington guns" that had been captured at Yorktown on October 19, 1781.

Though no one knows how the recipe originated, Chatham Artillery Punch probably fueled these occasions. Chatham members believe that the gentle ladies made the first batch. Then, one by one, Artillery officers added their own ingredients. Drink it if you dare. The Chatham Artillery Punch recipe is reprinted courtesy of the Savannah Area Convention & Visitor's Bureau.

1½ gallons catawba wine	½ gallon rum
1 quart gin	1 quart brandy
½ pint Benedictine	2 quarts maraschino cherries
1½ quarts rye whiskey	1½ gallons strong tea
2½ pounds brown sugar	1½ quarts orange juice
1½ quarts lemon juice	

Mix 36 to 48 hours before serving. Add one case of champagne when ready to serve.

Brunswick Stew

Brunswick Stew was created in Brunswick, Georgia. Serve with barbecue or seafood, such as boiled or fried shrimp, oysters, or crabs, from local waters. Makes one gallon.

1 3-pound chicken	1 pound lean pork
1 pound lean beef	3 medium onions, chopped

Place meat in large, heavy pot. Season with salt and pepper. Add onions and cover with water. Cook until meat falls from bones (several hours). Remove from heat and allow to cool. Tear meat into shreds and return to stock.

Add:
4 cans (16 oz.) tomatoes
5 tablespoons Worcestershire sauce
1½ bottles (14 oz.) catsup
1 tablespoon Tabasco
2 bay leaves
½ bottle (12 oz.) chili sauce
½ teaspoon dry mustard
½ stick butter
Cook one hour, occasionally stirring to prevent sticking.

Add:
3 tablespoons vinegar
2 cans (16 oz.) small lima or butter beans
2 cans (16 oz.) cream-style corn
1 can (15 oz.) small English peas
(3 small Irish potatoes, diced, and a box of frozen sliced okra—optional)
Cook slowly until thick.

Low Country Boil

½ pound cooked smoked sausage (kielbasa) per person
½ pound shrimp (in shell) per person
1 ear corn (shucked) per person
1 box shrimp boil per 2 pounds shrimp
1 teaspoon vinegar per pound shrimp
½ teaspoon Tabasco per pound shrimp
1 teaspoon red pepper per 4 pounds shrimp
1 teaspoon black pepper per 4 pounds shrimp
2 onions per person (optional)
3 new potatoes per person (optional)

Fill a large pot about three-quarters full of water. Add potatoes and all spices, bring to a boil, and cook five minutes.

Add sausage and bring back to boil for five minutes. Add onions and boil five minutes. Add corn and boil five minutes.

Check all ingredients for doneness, especially potatoes. Add shrimp and boil until shells begin to separate from the shrimp.

Turn off heat and let stand for a few minutes. Drain and serve.

Brunswick Stew and Low Country Boil recipes are reprinted by permission of the Brunswick & the Golden Isles Visitors Bureau.

More Recipes

Chicken Pita

This healthful sandwich is good served hot or cold with fresh fruit. It is reprinted courtesy of the Georgia Poultry Federation and Georgia Dietetic Association.

1 pound skinless, boneless chicken breasts, cut into chunks
2 cloves garlic, minced
1 medium onion, chopped
8 ounces fresh mushrooms, sliced
1 tablespoon chopped fresh tarragon (½ teaspoon dried)
⅓ cup plain non-fat yogurt
⅓ cup reduced calorie mayonnaise
½ cup chopped celery
¼ cup minced green onions
salt and pepper to taste
5 ounces fresh spinach, washed and dried
4 six-inch pita breads, cut in half

Place chicken, garlic, and onions in a two-quart casserole and sprinkle with tarragon. Cover and microwave on high for five minutes, or until juices run clear. Stir and add mushrooms. Cover and microwave on high for four to five minutes longer. Drain. Stir in yogurt, mayonnaise, celery, onions, salt, and pepper. Fill pita pockets with fresh spinach leaves and chicken mixture. Makes eight servings.

Roasted Georgia Grouper with Peanuts

1½ cups stone-ground wheat crackers
½ cup grated Romano cheese
¼ cup fresh parsley, chopped
½ teaspoon white pepper
¼ cup toasted peanuts
⅓ cup creamy peanut butter
1 tablespoon soy sauce
2 dashes red pepper
1 tablespoon fresh lemon juice
½ teaspoon garlic, pared and minced
½ cup chicken broth
2 large eggs
¼ cup water
2 tablespoons creamy peanut butter

Roasted Georgia Grouper

Peanut Advisory Board

¼ cup vegetable oil
2 tablespoons fresh lemon juice
6 grouper fillets, 6 ounces each

Combine stone-ground crackers, Romano cheese, parsley, pepper, and roasted peanuts in food processor. Process into crumbs. Pour crumbs into shallow bowl; reserve. Combine peanut butter, soy sauce, red pepper, lemon juice and garlic in food processor. Slowly add chicken broth while processing. Scrape sides and continue processing briefly. Set sauce aside at room temperature. Combine eggs, oil, water, 2 tablespoons lemon juice, and 2 tablespoons creamy peanut butter in food processor. Process to mix well. Pour into shallow bowl. Preheat oven to 450 degrees Fahrenheit. Rinse fillets and pat dry. Cut fillets into six strips each. Dip each fillet strip first into prepared egg wash, then pat into peanut crumbs. Arrange on non-stick baking sheet. Bake in upper third of oven five to ten minutes, or until golden and cooked through. Serve at once with peanut sauce. Makes 12 appetizer servings.

Southern Peanut Soup with Pepper Jelly

2 tablespoons butter
2 tablespoons onion, grated
1 branch celery, thinly sliced
2 tablespoons flour
3 cups chicken broth
½ cup peanut butter, creamy
¼ teaspoon salt
1 cup light cream
2 tablespoons chopped roasted peanuts
½ cup hot-pepper jelly

Southern Peanut Soup

Melt butter in a saucepan over low heat; add onion and celery. Sauté for about five minutes. Add flour and mix until well blended. Stir in chicken broth and allow it to simmer for about 30 minutes. Remove from heat, strain broth. Stir the peanut butter, salt, and cream into the strained broth until well mixed. Serve hot. Garnish each serving with a teaspoon of chopped peanuts and a dollop of jelly. Makes four servings.

Roasted Georgia Grouper with Peanuts and Southern Peanut Soup with Pepper Jelly reprinted courtesy of the Peanut Advisory Board.

The All-American Drink

In 1886 Atlanta druggist John S. Pemberton started concocting formulas in a quest to develop a nonalcoholic cure for the common headache. After months of combining extracts of African kola nuts, coca leaves, and other ingredients, he developed a beverage. He called it Coca-Cola and marketed it as a "temperance drink" capable of curing a variety of afflictions from headaches to depression.

Initially, Coke was sold as syrup which had to be diluted with water. One day, a customer asked a drug store soda jerk to mix up a glass. When the clerk substituted soda water for tap water, the carbonated soft drink was born.

Coca-Cola contains 15 secret ingredients. It is sold in 160 nations and is consumed 250 million times a day. Headquartered in Atlanta, the Coca-Cola company is Georgia's most famous corporation, and the drink may well be America's most famous product.

Atlanta's World of Coca-Cola interprets the history of of the world-famous soft drink

The World of Coca-Cola is a three-story pavilion exhibiting more than 1,000 pieces of memorabilia on Coke's history. *FYI:* 55 Martin Luther King Jr. Dr., Atlanta; (404) 676-5151. **Pemberton House**, a Victorian cottage once owned by Coke's creator, contains a kitchen/apothecary shop with Coca-Cola exhibits. *FYI:* 11 W. Seventh St., Columbus; (706) 323-7979. The Coca-Cola sign on **Young Brothers' Pharmacy** dates to 1894 and has been authenticated by Coke as the first outdoor painted wall advertisement for the beverage. *FYI:* 2 W. Main St., Cartersville; (404) 382-4010.

World's Largest Drive-In

The Varsity, near Georgia Tech, has been an Atlanta institution for more than 60 years. The world's largest fast food drive-in restaurant has been dishing up hot dogs, hamburgers, french fries, and onion rings since 1928. *FYI:* 61 North Ave., N.W., Atlanta; (404) 881-1706.

Special Tastes

The Claxton Fruitcake Company bakes and distributes more than six million pounds of fruitcake annually. Free samples and tours are offered throughout the year; baking season is September through mid-December. *FYI:* Claxton; (912) 739-3441.

Callaway Gardens is known for its muscadine grapes and features them in everything from ice cream and sauces to Muscadine Toast. *FYI:* Callaway Gardens; (706) 663-2281; outside Georgia, (800) 282-8181.

Double Q Farms is Georgia's largest kiwi producer. It markets kiwi fruit and gourmet jams. *FYI:* 1475 Hwy. 26, Hawkinsville; (800) 732-5510.

In the community of **Colquitt**, a jelly is made from the juice of the mayhaw berry, a cranberry-sized fruit found in southwest Georgia swamps and bogs. *FYI:* (912) 758-2400.

Bringing College Knowledge to the Land

In 1914 Georgia governor and U.S. Senator Hoke Smith and South Carolinian Frank Lever co-authored national legislation that provided a direct link between rural farmers and their state universities. The Smith-Lever Act called for the United States Department of Agriculture and land-grant universities "to aid in diffusing among the people . . . useful and practical information on subjects relating to agriculture and home economics, and to encourage applications of the same." Thus college cooperative extension programs were born at the University of Georgia and throughout the country.

Wineries

Georgia's wine industry has enjoyed a rebirth in the 20th century. Call ahead for tastings, which are offered at select times.

Chateau Élan Winery is housed in a 16th-century style chateau and includes a golf course, a European-style full service spa with 14 unique rooms, and four restaurants. Free daily tours and tastings. *FYI:* 7000 Old Winder Hwy., Braselton; (404) 932-0900; outside Georgia, (800) 233-9463.

Chateau Élan hosts special events and winery tours with tastings

Chestnut Mountain Winery's 30 acres of trees, lawns, vineyards, and rose gardens encompass a sampling room, picnic area, and nature trails. *FYI:* I-85, Exit 48, Braselton; (404) 867-6914.

Fox Winery offers daily tours and tastings. *FYI:* Covington; (404) 787-5402.

Habersham Vineyards and Winery's award winning wines can be sampled at their tasting rooms in Byron, Commerce, Dahlonega, Hiawassee, Roswell, and Underground Atlanta. *FYI:* (706) 778-9463.

Georgia Winery Taste Center and Outlet Store provides samples of Georgia peach wine and muscadine champagne. *FYI:* Near Stockbridge at I-75, Exit 141.

Old Sautee Store, in Helen, contains one of Georgia's largest collections of general store memorabilia

Learning the Land

You can learn more about Georgia agriculture by spending your vacation on a farm or visiting an attraction which interprets farm life. On **Georgia Farm Vacations and Tours**, activities may include swimming, fishing, horseback riding, hunting, exploring nature trails, vegetable gardening, and watching the planting, growing, and harvesting. *FYI:* (404) 656-3590 for directory.

Georgia Agrirama is a museum of a late 1800s farm community, including a one-room school, a water-powered grist mill, and a turpentine still.

FYI: I-75, Exit 20, Tifton; (912) 386-3344. **General Coffee State Park** exhibits a Pioneer Village, with agricultural artifacts plus outdoor recreational facilities. *FYI:* Six miles east of Douglas on GA 32; (912) 384-7082. **Hofwyl-Broadfield Plantation** demonstrates how rice was produced in coastal Georgia before the Civil War. *FYI:* National Park Service, Brunswick; (912) 264-9263.

Farmer's Markets

Atlanta State Farmer's Market: The largest farmer's market in the United States and second largest in the world offers fresh fruit and vegetables year-round. *FYI:* I-75, Forest Pkwy. Exit, Jonesboro; (404) 366-6910.

Your DeKalb Farmer's Market: The world's largest indoor market of its kind features fresh foods and baked goods from more than 30 countries. *FYI:* 3000 E. Ponce de Leon Ave., Decatur; (404) 377-6400.

Tasteful Events

Georgia Peanut Festival, October, recognizes the number one cash crop with a week-long event. *FYI:* Sylvester; (912) 776-6657.

Thunderbolt Seafood Harvest Festival, July, celebrates this historic fishing village with food, games, entertainment. *FYI:* 2092 River Dr., Savannah; (912) 355-4422.

Southern Wild Game and Fish Cookoff, March, features exhibits, arts and crafts, and entertainment, in Vienna. *FYI:* I-75, Exit 36; (912) 268-8275.

Taste of the Old South, May, Stone Mountain, features entertainment and demonstrations. Georgia peach cobbler, beach dances, crawfish races. *FYI:* Stone Mountain Park; (404) 498-5702.

Big Pig Jig, a week long October celebration, is the official Georgia Barbecue Cooking Championship and is rated one of America's top 100 events by the American Business Association and the Southeast Tourism Society. Includes a 5K "Hog Jog" run and $10,000 in prizes. *FYI:* I-75, Exit 36, Vienna; (912) 268-8275.

Watermelon Days Festival, July, includes watermelon-eating and seed-spitting contests, Old Fashioned Farm Day, and a gospel sing. *FYI:* Cordele; (912) 273-1668.

Peanut farming the old-fashioned way

Peanut Advisory Board

STATE OF THE ARTS

Georgia's mountains, red clay hills, rivers, and marshes have served as both inspiration and springboards to immortality for many poets, writers, musicians, and actors. "John Henry" and other folk songs originated in the Blue Ridge Mountains. "Fa-so-la" singing, which utilizes only four of the scale's seven notes, is a traditional folk music unique to northern Georgia.

Stephen Foster immortalized Okefenokee Swamp's Suwannee River in "Old Folks at Home"

The Atlanta Ballet is America's oldest ballet company. In the mid-1800s, Edwin Booth and his soon-to-be-infamous brother, John Wilkes Booth, performed Shakespeare in Georgia, while poet Sidney Lanier sang the praises of the marshes of Glynn and the Chattahoochee River.

A century later, country singer Alan Jackson had one of his biggest hits with a song called "Chattahoochee." Georgia has been a mecca for rock 'n' roll since the 1950s, and its scenery has been showing up more and more on motion picture and television screens in the 1980s and 1990s.

The Poetry Society of Georgia is one of the nation's oldest literary societies. The state has immortalized its artists by naming lakes and erecting monuments to poets, building bridges and boulevards to honor singers, and establishing halls of fame to commemorate entertainers. Little wonder, then, that all of the arts flourish and thrive, from the coast's white sand beaches to the Appalachian Highland's peaks.

Performing Arts

The Grammy Award-winning Atlanta Symphony performs more than 230 concerts annually. The Savannah Symphony stages summer concerts outdoors at Forsyth Park. Columbus Symphony presents 13 concerts per year and tours other cities, while Macon's stages host five classical and four pops concerts annually. Athens, Augusta, and Gainesville support symphonies. Most larger cities also have dance, choral groups, and live theater.

Grand Palaces

Georgia's theaters run the gamut from opulent historical palaces to modern multiplexes.

Atlanta's Fox Theatre, a 1929 Moorish/Egyptian/art deco palace listed on the National Register of Historic Places, hosts traveling Broadway shows and live performances

Kevin C. Rose, Atlanta Convention & Visitors Bureau

Callanwolde Fine Arts Center: This 1920 Tudor-style mansion, listed on the National Register, presents classical and contemporary concerts, recitals and dance, poetry readings, and theater. *FYI:* 980 Briarcliff Rd., N.E., Atlanta; (404) 872-5338.

Springer Opera House: Edwin Booth and Oscar Wilde trod its boards. It stages comedy, musicals, and drama, and hosts a ballet company and children's theater group. *FYI:* 103 10th St., Columbus; (706) 324-5714.

Imperial Community Theatre: Built in 1917, the theater once staged vaudeville shows and now presents plays, the Augusta Ballet, and the Augusta Opera. *FYI:* 745 Broad St., Augusta; (706) 722-8341.

Georgia Dept. of Industry and Trade

The Springer Opera House, in Columbus, is Georgia's official state theater and a National Historic Landmark

Rock 'n' Roll Forever

In the 1950s, when **"Little Richard" Penniman** stopped washing dishes in a Macon bus station and began shouting about "Tutti-Frutti," "Long Tall Sally," and "Lucille," he hit America with the subtlety of a blast furnace. Although the lyrics never made much sense, his flamboyance and cast-iron voice launched Georgia as a stronghold of rock and soul music.

James Brown got his start on a Macon radio station and was followed by **Gladys Knight** and **Curtis Mayfield**. Otis Redding became famous with "The Dock of the Bay" and other hits. During the 1970s, Macon-based Capricorn Records created a special niche for southern white rock by recording the **Allman Brothers Band**, the **Marshall Tucker Band**, and other groups.

In the 1970s and 1980s the **B-52s** and **R.E.M.** brought international fame to Athens. R.E.M.'s members hung out at Weaver D's Fine Foods Restaurant and used its motto, "Automatic For the People," as an album title. *FYI:* 1016 E. Broad St., Athens.

Augusta has honored James Brown with a boulevard. Macon's rock 'n' roll tour includes the Otis Redding Memorial Bridge and Library, Little Richard's boyhood home, the site of Capricorn recording studios, and Rose Hill Cemetery, the final resting place of Duane Allman and Berry Oakley of the Allman Brothers Band. The **Georgia Music Hall of Fame**, opening in 1996, honors more than 40 Georgia performers, including **Lena Horne**, **Johnny Mercer**, **Harry James**, **Bill Anderson**, and various rock stars. *FYI:* Macon-Bibb County Convention and Visitors Bureau; (912) 743-3401; outside Georgia, (800) 768-3401.

Lena Horne is honored in the Georgia Music Hall of Fame

Mother of the Blues

Gertrude "Ma" Rainey (1886–1939) inspired and influenced many later female singers and is often credited with being the first woman to incorporate blues into stage shows. Infidelity and the plights of southern blacks and white sharecroppers are common themes in the 100-plus songs she wrote and recorded. She was honored posthumously with a commemorative postage stamp, a 1993 Woman of Achievement Award, and induction into the Georgia Music Hall of Fame. Her home in Columbus is listed on the National Register of Historic Places. *FYI:* 805 Fifth Ave.

Florida State Archives

The legendary Ray Charles

The Genius

Ray Charles has been called an American icon and the genius of modern music. Born Ray Charles Robinson in Albany, Georgia, he was blind by age seven and an orphan at 15. As a pianist, saxophonist, singer, songwriter, and band leader, he has recorded rhythm and blues, soul, pop, rock, and jazz. "What'd I Say," a Hallelujah I Love Her So," "I Can't Stop Loving You," and "Georgia On My Mind" are among his many hits.

Blind Willie McTell (1901–1959)

Blues legend Blind Willie McTell was born and is buried at Thomson. An outstanding guitarist, he sang blues, rags, ballads, pop, and folk songs. He recorded for numerous labels without achieving commercial success. To supplement his income, he played traveling medicine shows, carnivals, and house parties, and sang on street corners. The Allman Brothers recorded his "Statesboro Blues," which became a favorite in their concerts. **The Blind Willie McTell Blues Festival**, in Thomson, honors him each autumn.

Country Music's Mecca

Buena Vista has become mecca for country music fans. The **Silver Moon Music Barn** offers name entertainers on weekends. *FYI:* Two miles south of Buena Vista on Hwy. 41; (800) 531-0677. Several museums exhibit entertainers' stage costumes, instruments, and personal effects. The **Elvis Presley Museum** has the world's largest private collection of Elvis memorabilia. *FYI:* Buena Vista; (912) 649-KING. The **National Country Music Museum**, housed in a 100-year-old cotton warehouse, exhibits more than 100 items once owned by Johnny Cash, Merle Haggard, Dolly Parton, Kenny Rogers, and others. *FYI:* Buena Vista; (800) 531-0677. The **Celebrity Collection** displays personal effects from Mohammad Ali, Sylvester Stallone, John Wayne, Barbra Streisand, and more than 90 other celebs. *FYI:* Front Porch Music Hall, Buena Vista; (912) 649-2028.

Art Museums

1) Georgia Museum of Art: The official state art museum contains more than 7,000 works, including 19th- and 20th-century American and Italian Renaissance paintings; and European, American, and Oriental prints and drawings. *FYI:* North University Campus, Athens; (706) 542-3255.

2) Madison Morgan Cultural Center: The Romanesque Revival red-brick building hosts 10–15 exhibits in four galleries, and 30–40 the-atrical performances annually. *FYI:* 434 S. Main St., Madison; (404) 342-4743.

3) Quinlan Arts Center: Traveling shows of Andy Warhol, Xavier Roberts, and others, plus regional and state artists are exhibited. *FYI:* U.S. 129 and GA 60, Gainesville; (404) 536-2595.

4) Marietta-Cobb Museum of Art: Permanent collections in this 1909 Greek Revival

Tourist Div., Ga. Dept of Industry & Trade

The 9,000-piece collection at Atlanta's High Museum of Art includes European/American paintings and sculpture, African art, 20th-century art, and photography

building showcase the 19th- and 20th-century American art of N.C. Wyeth, Robert Henri, and others. European art and exhibitions highlighting Western art movements also are included. *FYI:* 30 Atlanta St., N.E., Marietta; (404) 424-8142.

5) Michael C. Carlos Museum of Art and Archaeology: The Southeast's largest archaeological museum displays comprehensive collections of Egyptian, Greek, near Eastern, Columbian, and modern art. *FYI:* 571 S. Kilgo, Atlanta; (404) 727-4282.

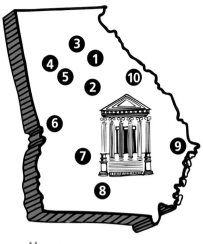

Museums

6) Chattahoochee Valley Art Museum: 20th-century American art is exhibited in a renovated 1892 jail. *FYI:* 112 Hines St., La Grange; (706) 882-3267.

7) Albany Museum of Art: One of the South's largest collections of traditional African Art is featured along with American and European 19th- and 20th-century creations. *FYI:* 311 Meadowlark Dr., Albany; (912) 439-8400.

8) Lowndes/Valdosta Cultural Arts Center: Painting, sculpture, group and individual shows, traveling exhibitions, and permanent collections are displayed. *FYI:* 1204 N. Patterson St., Valdosta; (912) 247-ARTS.

9) Telfair Academy of Arts and Sciences: The South's oldest art museum is housed in a mansion with an octagonal room and a rotunda gallery. Designed by William Jay in the early 1800s, it exhibits outstanding examples of American and European paintings and sculpture. *FYI:* 232 Barnard St., Savannah; (912) 232-1177.

Robert W. Woodruff Arts Center showcases the Atlanta Symphony Orchestra, theatrical productions, and visual arts

10) Morris Museum of Art: Multiple galleries exhibit Civil War art, black-influenced Southern art, and 20th-century and contemporary works. *FYI:* One 10th St. at Riverwalk, Augusta; (706) 724-5701.

Public Art

Public art comes in all shapes and sizes in Georgia, and honors everything from peanuts and poultry to Civil War battles and generals.

Confederate President Jefferson Davis and Generals Robert E. Lee and Stonewall Jackson are immortalized on Stone Mountain

Atlanta Convention and Visitor's Bureau

Stone Mountain

Georgia's top tourist attraction is also the world's largest bas-relief sculpture. The carved surface covers roughly three acres of Stone Mountain, measures 90 by 190 feet, and is recessed 42 feet into the mountain. Carvers took shelter from rain storms inside the horses' mouths. Carving started in 1923 and took more than 50 years to complete; it was interrupted by wars, lack of funds, and other problems. Sculptor Gutzon Borglum also carved Mount Rushmore. Augustus Lukeman designed the three figures, and Walker Kirkland Hancock completed them in 1972. *FYI:* 16 miles east of Atlanta on Hwy. 78; (404) 498-5633.

Atlanta Cyclorama

Listed on the National Register of Historic Places, the Cyclorama interprets the July 22, 1864, Battle of Atlanta. Completed in 1885, the painting-in-the-round is 400 feet in circumference and 50 feet high. It revolves around spectators as sound effects and narration highlight the battle. *FYI:* 800 Cherokee Ave., S.E., Atlanta; (404) 658-7625.

Atlanta Cyclorama

Georgia Dept. of Industry and Trade

Agricultural Art

Several Georgia towns honor the agricultural products that form the basis of their economy. Ashburn and Blakely have their peanut monuments. A three-foot-high bronze rooster tops a 25-foot-tall Georgia marble monument in Gainesville's Poultry Park, and a 56-foot-high sheet metal rooster advertises a Marietta fried chicken restaurant. Notable more for size than aesthetics, the iron chicken serves as a navigational aid for airline pilots and has inspired a "Gran Poulet" art festival, featuring works on a variety of birds.

Savannah's Waving Girl

Florence Martus was known worldwide as the "Waving Girl." According to legend, she greeted every ship that entered Savannah's port between 1877 and 1931 by waving a white handkerchief during the day and a lantern at night. Various theories say that her lover may have been lost at sea, or that he had sailed away, and she kept waiting for his return. Her statue is near the Ships of the Sea Museum.

New Deal Art

Between 1934 and 1943 some 1,000 post offices throughout the nation sported paintings and sculptured reliefs created as part of a federally sponsored program. Most are contemporary scenes depicting workers, town and country panoramas, and local historical events. *New Deal Art In Georgia*, a brochure published by the Georgia Museum of Art, describes some 34 works and provides the addresses of the Georgia post offices in which they are displayed.

Purchasing Pottery

Mark of the Potter: A 60-year-old water-powered cornmeal grist mill serves as a studio for craftspeople who make jewelry, weavings, handblown glass, and wheel-thrown pottery. *FYI:* Hwy. 197, Clarkesville; (706) 947-3440.
Mockingbird Forge: A blacksmith, a glass blower, a potter, and a woodworker create their specialties in a 1900 depot. *FYI:* U.S. 441 at Farmington; (706) 769-7147.

Pottery is a long established craft in Georgia

Georgia Dept. of Industry and Trade

Literary Georgia

Georgia's writers have created some of America's most important and enduring literature. Margaret Mitchell's *Gone With the Wind*, Erskine Caldwell's sharecroppers, and the grotesque, lonely misfits of Carson McCullers and Flannery O'Connor have shaped our perceptions of the South.

Sidney Lanier (1842–1881)

Sidney Lanier was born in Macon and attended Atlanta's Oglethorpe College, where he was inspired by the works of Scott, Tennyson, and Byron. "Song of the Chattahoochee" and "The Marshes of Glynn" reflect his love of Georgia and his passion for music. He died at age 39 of the tuberculosis he contracted in the Civil War.

Lake Sidney Lanier and Lanier County are named after him. Lanier Oak in Brunswick overlooks the marshes of Glynn. The Macon law office where he practiced with his father and uncle is preserved at 336-48 Second St.

Margaret Mitchell (1900–1949)

Atlanta newspaper reporter Margaret Mitchell recuperated from a back injury by writing a novel called *Tomorrow is Another Day*. It

Georgia Dept. of Industry and Trade

Sidney Lanier Cottage, in Macon, is an excellent example of 1840s Victorian architecture

was based partly on stories told by relatives whose ancestors had suffered losses in the Civil War. For several years, Mitchell reportedly used portions of the manuscript to prop up uneven tables. Retitled *Gone With The Wind*, it was published in 1936 and went on to win the Pulitzer Prize and become one of the best loved novels of all time.

The 1939 film won the Academy Award for best picture and remained Hollywood's top grossing movie for decades.

The writer's birthplace, **Margaret Mitchell House**, is located at 10th and Crescent Ave., Atlanta. *FYI:* (404) 870-2360. **Road to Tara Museum**, Atlanta, has the largest public exhibit of *Gone With*

Many believe that the description of Tara in Gone With the Wind *was based on this mansion at Lovejoy Plantation, near Jonesboro*

the Wind memorabilia. *FYI:* 659 Peachtree, #600, Atlanta; (404) 897-1939. Jonesboro and Clayton County provided the inspiration for the novel. *FYI:* Clayton County Convention Bureau; (800) 662-7829.

Lasting Impact

Erskine Caldwell (1903–1987): Born in Moreland, Georgia, Caldwell was the first southern writer to address social and economic conditions in the rural South. His 40 books of fiction, non-fiction, and short stories include *Tobacco Road* and *God's Little Acre*.

Carson McCullers (1917–1967): The Columbus writer's sensitive portrayals of loneliness live on in *The Heart is a Lonely Hunter* and *The Member of the Wedding*.

Flannery O'Connor (1925–1964): Using complex symbolism and violent, disturbed characters, O'Connor explored the themes of hypocrisy and cruelty in *A Good Man is Hard To Find*, *Everything That Rises Must Converge*, and other stories. Georgia College, in Milledgeville, houses her manuscripts, personal library, and furnishings. Her childhood home is at 207 E. Charlton St., Savannah; (912) 233-6014.

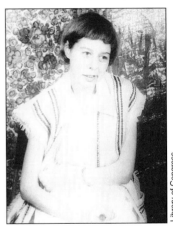

Carson McCullers

Georgia Literary Quiz

1) This novel, set in Civil War Georgia, won the 1956 Pulitzer Prize.
   a. *The Killer Angels*   b. *Andersonville*   c. *Tap Roots*
2) Alice Walker, Pulitzer Prize winner for *The Color Purple*, is from:
   a. Eatonton   b. Moultrie   c. Cochran
3) This town's 19th- and 20th-century commercial buildings inspired the setting for Olive Ann Burns' novel *Cold Sassy Tree*.
   a. Milledgeville   b. Sandersville   c. Commerce

ANSWERS: 1) b 2) a 3) c

Filming Georgia

If parts of Georgia look familiar, chances are you've seen them on film or television. Burt Reynolds and Jon Voight canoed down the milder stretches of the wild and scenic Chattooga River in *Deliverance.* Juliette's Whistle Stop Cafe appeared in *Fried Green Tomatoes. Glory's* assault on Fort Wagner was filmed on Jekyll Island. Crawfordville has often been a location for film and television productions, and the TV series *In the Heat of the Night* spent six seasons filming in Covington.

Several movie and TV stars hail from Georgia. Actress Kim Basinger grew up near Braselton and later bought the town. Susan Hayward lived in Carroll County during her career and considered it her home. Her gravesite is at Our Lady of Perpetual Care Catholic Church in Carrollton. *FYI:* (800) 292-0871.

Oliver Hardy (1892–1957)

Georgia's most famous actor may be comedian Oliver Hardy. Born in Harlem, Georgia, he hit the road at age eight as a soprano singer with traveling minstrel shows, then moved to Madison where his parents managed a hotel. By age 18 he had attended the Georgia Military Academy, studied law at the University of Georgia, and opened Milledgeville's first movie theater. After three years as manager, he joined a movie company as a comic villain. In 1926 he was teamed with Stan Laurel, and they went on to appear together in more than 100 motion pictures. After their film career ended, Laurel and Hardy continued to perform on stage, radio, and television. Film historians have called them the greatest comedy team of all time. Harlem's annual **Oliver Hardy Festival** includes a Laurel and Hardy movie marathon, impersonators, and a Hardy look-alike contest.

CNN

Atlanta-based Cable News Network (CNN) and Headline News are two 24-hour all-news networks operated by Turner Broadcasting System. On tours visitors can see the high-tech, fast paced, state-of-the-art international news operation from overhead walkways. *FYI:* One CNN Center, Marietta St. at Techwood Dr., Atlanta. Call ahead for tours; (404) 827-2300.

CNN Center

Kevin C. Rose, Atlanta Convention & Visitors Bureau

Events

Georgia Mountain Fair: Nashville stars, mountain folk musicians, a cloggers convention, and demonstrations of wood carving and moonshine stilling are featured. *FYI:* Hiawassee; (706) 896-4191.

Athens Jazz Festival: Wynton Marsalis and other major performers have headlined previous festivals at Athens' University of Georgia and local clubs during April and May.

Savannah Jazz Festival: A free festival with national jazz entertainers is held each September in Forsyth Park. *FYI:* Coastal Jazz Association; (912) 232-2222.

DeKalb International Choral Festival: Choral groups from 16 nations gather for five days of musical and cultural activities. *FYI:* DeKalb Convention and Visitors Bureau; (800) 999-6055.

Powers Crossroads County Fair and Art Festival: This Labor Day weekend festival consistently ranks as one of top 100 events in the nation. *FYI:* 12 miles southwest of Newnan on GA Hwy. 34; (404) 253-2011.

Arts-on-the-River: Savannah's visual and performing artists are showcased in juried art exhibits and performances by symphonies and ballet and theater companies. *FYI:* Savannah; (912) 651-6417.

BUILDING GEORGIA

Whether you're a casual or serious student of architecture, a trip through Georgia offers an unbroken record of every style, combination, and variation from the 1700s through today's state-of-the-art construction. In Georgia love of tradition and the elements of classical architecture has resulted in the preservation of complete towns as National Historic Districts—even multiple historic districts within larger communities.

Georgia Dept. of Industry and Trade

Thomson's Rock House dates to 1785 and is one of Georgia's oldest buildings

The first English and Scottish settlers carefully planned their towns and plantations. They platted them with precise grids of wide streets interspersed with parks and gardens. As later settlers migrated into Georgia from the northeastern United States, their communities reflected New England influences.

Although log cabins often predominated in other early settlements, many Georgia communities lacked the haphazard appearance of frontier towns and made a graceful transition into 19th-century sophistication.

Many consider the period from the late 1700s to the 1850s to be the golden age of Georgia architecture. While Georgia has a wealth of Federal, and Greek and Gothic Revival buildings, colonial homes are relatively few and were built mostly in older communities. The Civil War virtually halted construction of both homes and commercial buildings.

After the war, the state entered the Victorian age with gusto. Northern millionaires began wintering in Georgia and building opulent cottages. French and Italian Renaissance and Romanesque flourishes graced courthouses, churches, and other public buildings. The 1900s saw flirtations with Spanish Colonial and Beaux Arts styles, as well as innovations in design and use of space for commercial buildings and metropolitan areas.

Periods and Styles

Colonial, antebellum, and Victorian refer to time periods rather than styles. Colonial buildings were generally constructed between 1670 and 1820, "antebellum" refers to anything built prior to the Civil War, and the Victorian period lasted roughly from 1840 to 1900. Several styles evolved during each period. Through modifications, buildings and historic districts may exhibit a variety of elements representing numerous styles. The most important styles and their characteristics are:

The romantic Old South lives on in the antebellum homes and flower bedecked gardens of small Georgia towns such as Newnan

Federal, 1785–1840: Named because it was popular during the early days of the nation. Generally features symmetrical, low pitched roofs; circular or octagonal-shaped rooms.

Greek Revival, 1820–1860: Characterized by a two-story colonnade of four or six columns across the front; broad verandas; high ceilings.

Gothic Revival, 1835–1890: Features pointed arches; steeply gabled roofs; lacy details.

Victorian Period, 1840–1900: Encompasses many styles; adopted parts of Italian, French, English, Oriental, and Greco-Roman designs.

Italianate, 1845–1885: Inspired by Renaissance palaces and villas, buildings often include a tower or cupola; a two-story L- or T-shaped floor plan; and cast iron balconies.

Second Empire, 1855–1885: Name comes from France and the reign of Napoleon III (1852–1870). Steeply pitched mansard roofs with dormer windows are hallmarks.

Queen Anne, 1880–1910: Most popular Victorian style. Features irregular roof lines; steep gables; wrap-around porches; towers; stained and beveled glass; copious gingerbread trim.

Colonial Revival, 1880–1920: Embellished with Greek and Georgian details; classical columns on partially enclosed porches.

Classic Revival, 1880–1930: Fluted columns on front and sides of buildings; pillars have Corinthian capitals.

Bungalow, 1890–1930: Variation on Queen Anne cottage. Usually features one or two stories and a wide front porch with a low, gently sloping and gabled roof. Entrance directly into living room.

Tough Tabby

Spanish missionaries and Georgia's founders constructed many coastal towns of tabby, a cement-like material unique to the southern coast. Tabby mortar was made by grinding burned oyster shells into lime, then mixing with equal parts of sand and water. Whole oyster shells were added to serve as a binding agent. Because of its durability and the wide availability of the raw materials required to make it, tabby was used as a building material into the 1800s. Tabby forts constructed during the War of 1812 remained standing into the 20th century.

Fort Frederica displays ruins of the fort, barracks, homes, and other structures. *FYI:* Frederica Rd., St. Simons Island; (912) 638-3639. The remains of Georgia's first brewery and Hollybourne, a

Tabby mortar, a popular Georgia construction material, was made from ground oyster shells

cottage built in 1890, are weathering away on Jekyll Island's north end. The coast's best-preserved structures are **McIntosh Sugar Mill Ruins**, near St. Marys. Foundations and walls of rooms used for cane grinding, boiling, and processing sugar products still stand. Because they were used by both the Spanish and the English, the origins of some ruins are debatable. Some historians believe they were former Spanish missions, while others argue they are old sugar mills built between 1815 and 1825.

Savannah Elegance

Savannah's 2.2 square mile National Historic Landmark District is one of the largest, most highly acclaimed preservation areas in the United States. More than 1,400 buildings have been restored and are used as homes, churches, shops, and offices. Federal, Regency, 19th-century classical, Second Empire, and Victorian styles are all exhibited. The first to be preserved was the **Juliette Gordon Low Birthplace**, which was the family home of the Girl Scouts' founder. The Regency style home was built between 1818 and 1821 and features Egyptian Revival and classical details, with a Victorian garden. *FYI:* 142 Bull St.; (912) 233-4501.

Savannah's National Historic District includes 21 half-acre parks platted by founder James Oglethorpe, each with a central fountain or monument

Tourist Division, Georgia Dept. of Industry and Trade

Isle of Hope is a community of privately owned antebellum era homes, surrounded by moss-draped live oaks, magnolias, and azaleas. Some were built during early the 1800s as summer residences. They sit on a high bluff overlooking the Skidaway River near Savannah. *FYI:* Savannah Convention & Visitors Bureau; (912) 944-0456; outside Georgia, (800) 444-CHARM.

William Jay

After migrating from England by way of the West Indies, 23-year-old William Jay came to Savannah in 1817 to visit his sister. Although he stayed only eight years, he designed many of Savannah's homes. They reflect the elegance of his native Bath, as well as his English residences in the West Indies. He left in 1825, but his designs influenced future architects for decades. Savannah's **Owens-Thomas House** and the **Green-Meldrim House**, both designed by Jay, are outstanding examples of 19th-century Regency row houses. The latter belonged to a wealthy cotton planter and was General Sherman's headquarters during his occupation of Savannah.

English Influences

Clinton was settled by New Englanders in 1808 and became a 19th-century county seat. While it was the scene of Civil War battles, raids, and occupations by both Confederate and Union troops, it has survived free of modern development. Its gridiron pattern, with streets named after Revolutionary War heroes, give it the appearance of an early New England town. Old Clinton Historic District preserves 12 houses constructed between 1808 and 1830 and the Methodist Church, built in 1821. *FYI:* 12 miles northeast of Macon, west of U.S. Hwy. 129; (912) 986-3384.

Plantation Plain

Slaves working in the fields of large plantations and magnificent mansions surrounded by whitewashed columns and broad porches are often thought of as symbols of the pre-Civil War South. These scenes, however, were the exception rather than the rule.

By 1860 there were 591,550 people living in Georgia. About 41,000 were slaveholders. Approximately 6,000 owned more than 20 slaves; the vast majority had fewer than five. Georgia's poorest whites lived little better than black slaves.

Jarrell Plantation, near Juliette, exemplifies the typical Georgia

Georgia Dept. of Industry and Trade

farm. It includes a steam powered mill, a carpenter shop, a three-story barn, a cane furnace, a syrup mill, and a blacksmith shop. The plantation houses one of the largest and most complete collections of original family artifacts of the period. *FYI:* Jarrell Plantation Rd., eight miles southeast of Juliette; (912) 986-5172.

Jarrell Plantation exhibits 20 historic buildings constructed between 1847 and 1945

After 1800 the wealthiest plantations became the South's largest and most powerful economic and social institutions. In Georgia most large plantations were situated in the northeastern, middle, and southern regions. These self-contained agricultural entities required hundreds of acres to grow cotton, sugar, rice, tobacco, and other crops to feed slaves and cattle. As owners prospered, many built townhouses in nearby communities.

Old South Architecture

The Antebellum Trail (U.S. 129/GA 22/U.S. 441 east of I-75) winds south from Athens, through Georgia's heartland, and into several towns. The trail passes magnificent pre-Civil War mansions, plantation homes, and magnolia-shaded formal gardens. *FYI:* For brochure, contact: Antebellum Trail, P.O. Box 656, Eatonton, GA 31024; (706) 485-7707.

Most of the towns along the route survived the Civil

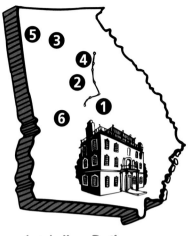

Antebellum Trail

War intact. They include Watkinsville, Madison, Eatonton, Milledge-ville, Clinton, and Macon. In addition to the Federal, and Greek and Gothic Revival buildings of the antebellum period, many towns also exhibit Victorian Italianate, Second Empire, Queen Anne, Colonial Revival, Classic Revival, and Bungalow styles.

Classic Cities

1) Milledgeville: The National Trust for Historical Preservation considers Georgia's antebellum capital the only surviving example of a complete Federal-period city. Except for Washington, D.C., it is the only U.S. town designed as a capital city. The white-columned **Old Governor's Mansion** is a perfect example of Greek Revival architecture. It served as the executive mansion from 1839 to 1868. *FYI:* (912) 453-4545. The **Old State Capitol Building**, built in 1807, was one of the earliest public buildings in the United States constructed in neo-Gothic style. It has housed the Georgia Military College since 1880 and is recognized as a last citadel of the Old South. *FYI:* (912) 454-2700.

Georgia Dept. of Industry and Trade

The Lapham-Patterson mansion, Thomasville, is an outstanding example of Queen Anne architecture

More Classic Cities

2) Madison: The National Register District in Madison is one of oldest and largest in the state. It was spared the torch when U.S. Senator Joshua Hill, a friend of Sherman's brother, met with the general and persuaded him to leave it intact. It was once described as "the most cultured and aristocratic town on the stage coach route from Charleston to New Orleans." Most of Madison's buildings were constructed between 1830 and 1860. Styles represented include Federal, Greek Revival with Italianate embellishment, Tudor, Queen Anne, Second Empire, and Romanesque Revival. Some are considered among the finest examples in the state. *FYI:* Chamber of Commerce; (706) 342-4454.

3) Roswell: The Roswell town square reflects New England influences. Fifteen homes and storefronts, dating to 1839, represent the entire social class spectrum— from wealthy mill owners and farmers to factory managers and illiterate mill workers. Greek Revival **Bulloch Hall** was the home of Theodore Roosevelt's mother and Eleanor Roosevelt's grandmother. **Archibald Smith Plantation Home**, including 13 outbuildings, was constructed in 1845 and is preserved in its original state. It accurately suggests the southern lifestyle of a mid-19th-century cotton planter. *FYI:* Chamber of Commerce; (404) 640-3253.

Roswell has some of the nation's oldest apartments. Built around 1840 as homes for mill workers, two buildings known as "the Bricks" contain ten apartments with hand-planed floors and original square nails. Each unit had a kitchen/living room on the first floor and a steep stairway to an upstairs bedroom. The Roswell Founders Club, a social and entertainment center, is housed in the Bricks Building. *FYI:* Roswell Convention and Visitors Bureau; (404) 640-3253.

4) Athens: Most architectural styles from the Federal through the Victorian era are represented in Athens. They include the **Church-Waddel-Brumby House**, built in 1820; the **Joseph Henry Lumpkin House**, an 1841 Greek Revival

Greater Rome Convention & Visitors Bureau

Martha Berry Museum and Art Gallery is a magnificent example of Greek Revival architecture and includes one of the Rome area's finest art collections

The Ford Complex on Berry College campus

Greater Rome Convention and Visitors Bureau

structure; and an 1857 home with 14 Corinthian columns on the front and sides, Doric columns at rear, and a five-acre garden. *FYI:* Athens Convention & Visitors Bureau; (404) 546-1805.

5) Rome: The town includes a restored Victorian river district and many examples of adaptive restoration which are on the National Register. **Oak Hill**, a classic antebellum plantation, was the home of Martha Berry, founder of Berry College. Manicured lawns, giant oak trees, and several gardens surround it. *FYI:* 189 Mount Berry Station, Mount Berry; (706) 291-1883. On the 26,000-acre **Berry College** campus, seven English Gothic buildings funded by Henry Ford form a quadrangle around a beautiful reflecting pool. *FYI:* Rome Convention and Visitors Bureau; (706) 295-5576; outside Georgia, (800) 444-1834.

6) Macon: A variety of architecture is exhibited in six National Historic Districts. The **Hay House**, an Italianate Renaissance Revival masterpiece, took five years to complete. Built in 1860, its 18,000 square feet encompass 24 rooms, 19 marble mantels, elaborate embossed cornices, exquisite plasterwork, and stained glass. *FYI:* 934 Georgia Ave., Macon; (912) 742-8155. **The Woodruff House**, built in 1836, was the home of one of the South's wealthiest cotton planters and the scene of a ball for Jefferson Davis' daughter. *FYI:* 988 Bond St., (912) 744-2715.

Victorian Extravagance

In the late 1800s some of the world's wealthiest people discovered southern Georgia's balmy winter climate.

Thomasville's Pebble Hill Plantation

Georgia Dept. of Industry and Trade

Thomasville was founded in the 1820s, and exploded with elegant cottages when it became a center for winter quail hunting between 1870 and 1906. Since tastes and wealth varied, virtually every style of architecture is preserved in seven historic districts. The town of 20,000 people is also famous for its lawns adorned with roses, pink and white dogwoods, and azaleas.

Pebble Hill Plantation, built in the 1820s, became the Georgian and Greek Revival centerpiece of a sprawling shooting plantation. It is the only plantation open to the public and displays horse and hound portraits, 33 original Audubon prints, antiques, and Indian artifacts. Visitors can tour stables and kennels, a carriage house with vintage automobiles, a reflecting pond, and formal gardens. *FYI:* U.S. 319 South, Thomasville; (912) 226-2344. The **Lapham-Patterson House**, circa 1885, is an outstanding example of Queen Anne resort architecture. Built as a winter cottage for a shoe merchant who was nearly killed in the great Chicago fire, its 19 rooms contain 45 doors and no right angles. *FYI:* 626 N. Dawson St., Thomasville; (912) 225-4004.

Georgia Dept. of Industry and Trade

Jekyll Island's clubhouse, which once served as the focal point for millionaires' social activities, has been restored as a resort hotel

The World's Most Exclusive Club

In 1886, 100 of America's wealthiest industrialists bought Jekyll Island. Among them were J.P. Morgan, Vincent Astor, William F. Vanderbilt, Marshall Field, and the Goodyear, Rockefeller, and Pulitzer families. By 1900 their membership reportedly included more than one-sixth of the world's wealth. A 1904 edition of *Munsey's Magazine* called their retreat the most exclusive, most inaccessible club in the world. After building "cottages" and a large, turreted clubhouse, they spent the next 56 winters hunting, playing tennis and golf, and making sure "no unwanted foot ever stepped on the island." **Jekyll Island Club Historic District**, a National Historic Landmark, encompasses 240 acres and 33 mansion-sized cottages. Restored club buildings are open for tours. The Victorian clubhouse has been transformed into an elegant hotel with beach club, 63-hole golf course, indoor/outdoor tennis, and croquet. *FYI:* 375 Riverview Dr., Jekyll Island; (912) 635-2762.

Antiques

The **Antiques Trail** parallels portions of the Antebellum Trail. Approximately 100 dealers in nine communities offer genuine antiques and collectibles. *FYI:* Georgia Antiques Trail Association; (912) 743-3401.

Cave Spring: Numerous dealers and a variety of artisans create bronze castings, pottery, paintings, hand-painted porcelain, furniture reproductions, cast iron patio furniture, and carousel horses. *FYI:* City of Cave Spring; (404) 777-3382.

Atlanta Flea Market & Antique Center: Offers 80,000 square feet of antiques, collectibles, and gift items. *FYI:* I-285, Exit 23, on Peachtree Industrial Blvd.; (404) 458-0456.

Old Mill Antique Village: Antiques and furniture refinishing in a restored textile village. *FYI:* Near DeKalb Farmers Market, Scottsdale; (404) 292-0223.

Chamblee's Antique Row: Forty shops host more than 200 dealers in historic homes, churches, and stores. Specialties include furniture, glass, pottery, linens, quilts, primitives, and crafts. *FYI:* Broad St. and Peachtree Rd., Chamblee; (404) 458-1614.

Marietta: Twenty-one stores and galleries sell furniture, primitives, collectibles, pottery, and crystal. *FYI:* Visitors Information, (404) 429-1115.

Macon's Hay House contains priceless antiques

Tourist Division, Georgia Dept. of Industry and Trade

Atlanta's Modern Skyline

Atlanta architect John Portman has helped shape the city's dramatic modern skyline. It includes the Peachtree Plaza Hotel, which is the tallest hotel in the nation; and the world's first atrium style hotel, the Hyatt Regency Atlanta, which was built in 1967.

Atlanta's skyline reflects a variety of architectural influences, from classical to modern

Kevin C. Rose, Atlanta Convention & Visitors Bureau

Peachtree Center

In designing Peachtree Center, Portman said his idea was to create an "urban village where everything is in reach of the pedestrian." Spanning 11 blocks, it is a multi-dimensional complex of soaring towers, interior atriums, and exterior aerial walkways. *FYI:* Bound by Baker, Ellis, Williams, and Courtland Sts., N.E., Atlanta; (404) 659-0800.

Underground Atlanta

Two-thirds of Underground Atlanta is actually above the ground. The six city blocks of the urban marketplace include an historic district, three dozen restaurants and nightclubs, and more than 100 specialty shops. A turn-of-the-century town square with flickering street lights, balconies, and wrought iron fences provides a backdrop for brick-paved streets and early 1900s-style pushcarts. Peachtree Fountain Plaza features a 138-foot-tall light tower and three cascading fountains. *FYI:* 50 Upper Alabama St., Atlanta; (404) 523-2311.

The Swan House, a 1928 Palladian-style mansion, is part of the Atlanta Historical Society complex

Georgia Dept. of Industry and Trade

Herndon Home

Designed and built in 1910 by Alonzo F. Herndon, a former slave who founded the Atlanta Life Insurance Company, the home is an excellent example of Beaux Arts classical architecture. *FYI:* 587 University Pl., Atlanta; (404) 581-9813.

Gardens

State Botanical Garden of Georgia: The garden's 313 acres encompass 11 specialty gardens, five miles of nature trails, and a three-story conservatory with tropical and semitropical plants. *FYI:* 2450 S. Milledge Ave., Athens; (706) 542-1244.

Callaway Gardens: 14,000 acres of hills, meadows, lakes, and woodlands are filled with wildflowers, rhododendrons, and 700 varieties of azaleas. During the autumn chrysanthemum season, thousands of mums spread splashes of color over the hillsides. Floral displays change at the **John A. Sibley Horticultural Center**. The **Cecil B. Day Butterfly Center**, home to more than 1,000 butterflies, is North America's largest free-flight butterfly conservatory. The site also includes a 63-hole golf course, a tennis complex, a quail and deer hunting reserve, and a large man-made beach. *FYI:* (706) 633-2281; outside Georgia, (800) 282-8181.

Barnsley Gardens: Although the manor house is in ruins, 30 acres of gardens dating to 1840 have been restored and display daffodils, rhododendrons, and hundreds of roses. The green rose is unique to Barnsley Gardens, which also features fern, water, and bog gardens and a redwood arbor. *FYI:* 597 Barnsley Gardens Rd., Adairsville; (404) 773-7480.

Atlanta Botanical Garden: The garden and Fuqua Conservatory display 16,000 square feet of tropical, desert, and endangered plants, along with acres of hardwood trees, roses, azaleas, herbs, wildflowers, and a Japanese garden. *FYI:* Piedmont Park at The Prado; (404) 876-5858.

Atlanta Botanical Garden

Atlanta Convention & Visitors Bureau

Massee Lane Gardens: The American Camellia Society's headquarters offers nine acres of winter camellias followed by spring azaleas, dogwoods, narcissus, iris, and roses, plus a Japanese garden. Also on the garden site is the **Stevens-Taylor Gallery and Fetterman Museum**, which showcases the world's largest and most complete collection of Edward Marshall Boehm porcelains. *FYI:* Five miles south of Fort Valley; (912) 967-2722.

THE SPORTING LIFE

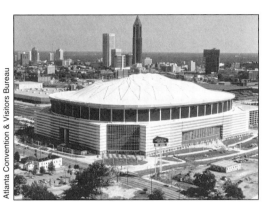

The Georgia Dome, home of the Atlanta Falcons, 1994 Super Bowl, and 1996 Olympic gymnastics and basketball

Going for the Gold

When the International Olympic Committee selected Atlanta as the host city for the 1996 Olympics, it marked the first time the summer games were held in the southern United States and east of the Mississippi River. State-of-the-art Olympic recreation and athletic facilities, to be used in the future for local spectator sports, are now part of the city's skyline.

By 1994, Atlanta was building an 85,000-seat Olympic Stadium, where the opening and closing ceremonies, football, and track and field would be held. It will become the home of the Atlanta Braves baseball team.

Because of its reliable racing conditions, Savannah was selected as the site for Olympic yachting. A new marina, a health spa, and a golf clubhouse were built at Savannah's Olympic Village, and additional rowing and canoeing facilities were installed at Lake Sidney Lanier.

Columbus built a softball complex for hosting the first-ever Olympic softball competition. Stone Mountain Park added a tennis center, an archery range, and the Velodrome, for cycling.

Pro Sports

The Atlanta Braves play baseball at Fulton County Stadium. *FYI:* 521 Capitol Ave.; (404) 249-6400 for tickets. Fans can cheer the Atlanta Hawks of the

The Atlanta Braves were National League champions in 1991 and 1992

NBA at the Omni Sports Arena. *FYI:* 100 Techwood Dr.; (404) 249-6400 for tickets. The NFL's Falcons play football in the Georgia Dome, site of the 1994 Super Bowl; visitors can watch select summer training practices at Falcons headquarters in nearby Suwannee. *FYI:* 2745 Burnette Rd.; (404) 945-1111.

Start Your Engines

Road Atlanta is the South's premier motor sports venue. Its 2.52 mile asphalt track is home to the Sports Car Club of America National Championship race. *FYI:* 5300 Winder Hwy., Braselton; (404) 967-6143. The **Atlanta Motor Speedway** hosts NASCAR Winston Cup stock car races, plus Busch Grand National, IMSA, and ARCA events. *FYI:* Hwy. 19-41 South, Hampton; tickets: (404) 946-4211; tours: (404) 707-7970.

Auto racing is a major sport in Georgia

Georgia Dept. of Industry and Trade

Golf and Tennis Anyone?

Professional golfers stop annually at Augusta National for The Masters; Mountain View Golf Course (Callaway Gardens) for the PGA Buick Southern Open; and Atlanta Country Club for the PGA Bell South Atlanta Golf Classic.

The state's 349 courses include 150 public and 41 municipal, plus five in state parks. Several public courses were designed by pros Jack Nicklaus, Arnold Palmer, Robert Trent Jones, Tom Weiskoph, and Gary Player. *Golf Digest* ranks **Jones Creek Golf Course**, Evans, second only to Augusta National, and calls it the best public course in the state. **Jekyll Island**'s first golf course was built by the millionaires' club. Four courses are open to all. From mid-November to early-February, fees are free with hotel room or cottage rentals. *FYI:* Jekyll Island Convention and Visitors Bureau; (912) 635-3636; outside Georgia, (800) 841-6586.

Jekyll Island Tennis Center received the U.S. Tennis Association's Outstanding Public Tennis Facility Award. *Tennis* magazine named it one of the nation's 25 best municipal facilities. *FYI:* (912) 635-3154.

The Masters

The Masters, the world's most prestigious golf tournament, is played each April amidst the flaming azaleas and blooming dogwoods of the Augusta National Golf Club. Although the U.S. Open, PGA, and British Open tournaments also attract golf's best players, none carries the Masters' mystique.

Brunswick and The Golden Isles Visitor's Bureau

Superb golf resorts are situated throughout the state

Founded in 1934 by Bobby Jones and Cliff Roberts, it has been played every year except 1943 through 1945. The first eight tournaments had an annual purse of $5,000, with $1,500 for the winner. Sam Sneed competed in a record 44 Masters, while Jack Nicklaus has the most wins with six. He also shot the highest and lowest winning scores of 288 (in 1966) and 271 (in 1965) and has averaged 67, or five under par, in 15 successive Masters. Arnold Palmer led the field a record 14 times.

The ceremonial green coat awarded to the winner may be worn only on Augusta National's grounds and cannot be used in commercial endorsements. Augusta National is a private club built on a former indigo plantation, and a National Registered Landmark.

Who Gets Invited?

To compete in The Masters you have to be invited. To be invited you have to demonstrate some mastery of golf. Invitations are extended to previous Masters' winners, the top 24 players in last year's Masters, and the last five U.S. Open, PGA, and British Open champions. Other invites go to major PGA tournament winners, the previous year's top 30 money winners, the top 16 players from the prior U.S. Open, and the top eight from the PGA. Three U.S. and British Amateur champions are also invited.

Georgia Sports Immortals

Bobby Jones (1902–1971): Born in Atlanta, Jones won 13 major golf tournaments before retiring at age 28. He is the only golfer to have won the "Grand Slam" of both Open and Amateur Championships in the United States and Great Britain in a single season.

Hank Aaron (b. 1934): Baseball's all-time home run leader played for the Atlanta Braves and broke 21 baseball records during his 23-year career. His 715th home run, hit on April 8, 1974, broke Babe Ruth's career record.

Ty Cobb (1886–1961): Born in Banks County and called the "Georgia Peach," Cobb won 12 batting titles. During his career with the Detroit Tigers (1906–26) and Philadelphia Athletics (1926–28), he compiled a record .367 lifetime batting average and a record 2,245 runs scored. In the 1915 season alone, he stole 96 bases; this record was not broken until 1962. Cobb was one of the first to be inducted into the Baseball Hall of Fame. Royston City Hall's **Ty Cobb Memorial** includes his memorabilia and a statue.

Jackie Robinson (1919–1972): Born in Cairo, Georgia, Robinson broke baseball's color barrier in 1947 to become the first black major leaguer. He won a National League batting title and a Most Valuable Player award.

Jim Brown (b. 1936): Born on St. Simons Island, Brown established himself as one of football's greatest players by running 12,312 yards in nine years with the Cleveland Browns.

Butts-Mehre Heritage Hall interprets Georgia sports history with 28 exhibits, Herschel Walker's Heisman trophy, and Fran Tarkenton's helmet. *FYI:* Lumpkin St. and Pinecrest Dr., Athens; (706) 542-9094.

Ty Cobb was known as the "Georgia Peach"

Camping Out

Woods, lakes, and streams in 45 state parks cover 60,000 acres in Georgia. Forty state parks offer camping. *FYI:* Georgia State Parks, (404) 656-3530. The Chattahoochee and Oconee National Forests offer camping, hiking, hunting, fishing, and boating. You can also pitch a tent or park a trailer at Lakes Sidney Lanier, Strom Thurmond, Oconee, Sinclair, and West Point. Many parks and resorts are bases for hikes into the surrounding countryside.

Black Rock Mountain State Park is a popular hiking spot

Hiking the High Country

Three of the state's most popular hikes include: 1) The **Appalachian Trail**, which starts in northwest Georgia and winds for 2,100 miles to Maine; 2) The **Bartram Trail**, blazed by Quaker naturalist William Bartram more than 200 years ago, which begins near Clayton and meanders through 40 miles of woodlands; and 3) **F. D. Roosevelt State Park**, at the southern end of the Appalachian Mountains, a year-round destination for hikers and horseback riders. The 23-mile Pine Mountain Trail, one of the Southeast's most popular hiking and backpacking routes, winds through the 10,000-acre park and passes two lakes. *FYI:* 2970 Hwy. 190 East, Pine Mountain, (706) 663-4858.

Cloudland Canyon hikes offer beautiful waterfalls and rugged country

Hunter's Paradise

In Georgia hunting is more than recreation. It is a way of life steeped in history. Thomasville's development is directly tied to the tradition and popularity of its quail hunting.

If it's wild and it walks or flies, chances are you can hunt it in Georgia. Rabbits, raccoons, opossum, squirrels, coyotes, bobcat, fox, deer, bear, and wild hogs are all fair game. So are crows, grouse, marsh hens, doves, ducks, geese, and wild turkey. In addition to guns, you can use archery equipment to hunt select game. You need a big game license in addition to a regular hunting or archery license for deer, turkey, and bear.

Wildlife Management Areas

Along with hunting, more than 70 wildlife management areas offer camping, canoeing, fishing, rock climbing, caving, and hiking at select sites. Some WMAs have shooting ranges for rifles; handguns and archery equipment are available for rent at select sites. All ranges are unstaffed. *FYI:* Georgia Department of Natural Resources, Wildlife Resources Division; (404) 918-6400, for seasons, regulations, and wildlife management areas information.

Plantation Pleasures

If you have plenty of money, you can hunt in grand style at several plantations. **Wild Ridge Plantation** leases its 2,500 acres to select groups and guests each year for classic quail hunts with dogs and handlers. *FYI:* P.O. Box 1337, Thomasville, GA 31799. **Myrtlewood Plantation** features a lodge, fishing, a sporting clays course, and classic plantation quail hunts. *FYI:* P.O. Box 32, Thomasville, GA 31799; (912) 228-6232. **Pine Hill Plantation** carries on the quest for quail with traditional hunts on horseback or by mule-drawn wagon. *FYI:* Colquitt; (912) 758-6602. **Quail Ridge Hunting Preserve** opens seasonally for large-group quail, dove, and duck hunts with jeep, foot, or mule-drawn wagon. *FYI:* Douglas; (912) 384-0025. **Addison Wild Boar Hunting** offers controlled boar hunts for guns and bow, with professional hounds and guides. *FYI:* One mile north of Addison on GA 87. **Cherokee Rose Shooting Resort** provides championship sporting clays, rifle and shotgun games, a shooting school, and rental shotguns. *FYI:* 895 Baptist Camp Rd., Griffin; (404) 228-2529.

At the Water's Edge

Among the favorite pastimes at the Georgia seashore are swimming, sunbathing, kite flying, and collecting shells. Bird and dolphin watching, crabbing, scuba diving, and snorkeling are popular seasonal pursuits. Jekyll Island, with ten miles of beach, has the most shoreline accessible by car. At Tybee Island you can walk along five miles of white sand beach fronting the Atlantic Ocean, take nature trails through maritime forests, and see an assortment of wildlife and birds. In addition to golf and tennis, the Jekyll Island Club Historic District encompasses fitness centers, water theme parks, and campgrounds near the beach. A 20-mile bicycle path weaves through the island's lush foliage. **Jekyll Island Historic Marina** offers deep sea fishing and sightseeing charters. *FYI:* N. Riverview Dr.; (912) 635-2891. At **Golden Isles Marina** visitors can charter boats for deep sea and river fishing, sightseeing, and sunset cruises, and rent Jet Skis and scuba diving equipment. *FYI:* (912) 634-1128. Visiting boaters will also find plenty of marinas and boat ramps in Savannah, Richmond Hill, Midway, Darien, Brunswick, and St. Marys.

Georgia Dept. of Industry and Trade

St. Simons Island combines beaches, unique history, elegant old hotels, and new resorts

Fishing the Deep

Georgia's coast attracts large numbers of big fish, both inshore and offshore, year-round. Summer brings king mackerel, bonita, dolphin, sea trout, and huge sea bass to join schools of tarpon and redfish. You can land your catch from boats, shoreline, or fishing piers.

King of the Sport Fish

In 1884 Samuel H. Jones of Philadelphia kicked off the sport of deep sea fishing by landing a seven foot, four inch long tarpon weighing 172½ pounds.

Tarpon are fast swimmers and make spectacular leaps out of the water as they attempt to free themselves from hooks. Because they grow to eight feet long and 340 pounds, and react violently when hooked, it usually takes an experienced angler to land them. One of the most primitive of the bony fishes, they are not considered good eating.

A female tarpon lays up to 12 million eggs. Mature tarpons have only one dorsal fin and large silvery scales which can measure two inches across. While they have well-developed gills, they must surface to gulp air. They live equally well in fresh and salt water. Although their natural habitat is the south Atlantic coast and tropical West Africa, they have been found as far north as Nova Scotia.

Lake and Stream Fishing

On June 2, 1932, George Washington Perry landed a world record 22 pound, 4 ounce largemouth bass on Montgomery Lake. Lake Seminole is considered one of the nation's best bass lakes, and the Altamaha River, the Ocmulgee River, Lake Sinclair, and Oconee Lake also stand out. Northern mountain lakes and streams are known for excellent trout fishing. Anglers return to southern Georgia waters for catfish, bass, bream, and shad.

Many wildlife management areas offer pond and lake fishing with a license and a WMA stamp. *FYI:* Georgia Department of Natural Resources, Wildlife Resources Division; (404) 918-6400.

On the Water

Paddling Georgia

Exploring Georgia by canoe, kayak, or raft can mean a leisurely outing or a thrilling white water adventure. Riding the **Chattahoochee River**—"Shootin' the Hooch," as locals say—is a tradition in the metro Atlanta area. The Chattahoochee Outdoor Center rents equipment. *FYI:* (404) 395-6851.

Augusta Canal, built in 1844, stretches for nine miles parallel to the Savannah River and flows by the Confederate Powder Works site. Adjacent Savannah Rapids Park is a departure point for canoeing and bicycling. *FYI:* Augusta Canal Authority, 1717 Goodrich St., (706) 722-1071. Savannah Rapids Park, 3300 Evans-to-Locks Rd., Martinez; (706) 868-3349.

Okefenokee and Grand Bay

Okefenokee Swamp offers 15 designated canoe trips ranging from 16 to 43 miles and lasting from two to four days each. Each trail is limited to one party daily, with a maximum of ten canoes and/or 20 people each. *FYI:* U.S. Fish and Wildlife Service, (912) 496-3331 for reservations. **Grand Bay**, second in size only to Okefenokee, totals 1,350 acres of man-made wetlands. A designated trail for canoes and outboards passes floating islands and a wading bird rookery. Wildlife includes alligators, blue and green-back herons, and the rare Florida water rat. *FYI:* Ten miles north of Valdosta on Hwy. 221; (912) 423-2988; outside Georgia, (800) 569-TOUR.

White Water Thrills

The Wild and Scenic **Chattooga River** drops some times gradually, sometimes dramatically along 50 miles of shear cliffs, magnificent waterfalls, and narrow canyons. Beginning and intermediate rafters ply the Class III section, and the Class IV portion poses the ultimate challenge for experienced rafters in good physical condition.

FYI: Nantahala Outdoor Center; (800) 232-7238. The **Oconee River**, near McCaysville, was selected for the 1996 Olympic white water events. It drops 246 feet in five miles of Class III and IV rapids. *FYI:* White Water Express; (800) 676-7238. The Flint River Outdoor Center rents equipment for shooting the Class I-III **Flint River** rapids. *FYI:* Thomaston; (706) 647-2633.

Lakeside Resorts and State Parks

Many resorts and state parks offer water based recreation. **Lake Lanier Islands** has two full-service resorts, each with 18-hole golf courses, water playgrounds, 300 lakeside camp-sites, fishing, bicycling, and horseback riding. *FYI:* 6950 Holiday Rd., Buford; (404) 932-7200. In 1928 auto manufac-turer Howard Coffin established the world famous **Cloister Resort** on Sea Island, with spas, nature programs, and activi-ties including golf, tennis, skeet shooting, sailing, fishing, and horseback riding. *FYI:* (800) SEA-ISLAND. **Hartwell Lake**, at 55,590 acres, is one of the Southeast's largest man-made reservoirs and a favorite of swimmers, fishermen, boaters, and campers. *FYI:* Hartwell; (706) 376-4788. **Hard Labor Creek State Park** at 5,805 acres, is Georgia's largest state park. You can rent a cottage, golf, camp, ride horses, and boat on 45-acre and 275-acre lakes. *FYI:* Two miles north of Rutledge; (404) 557-2863. **Reed Bingham State Park** surrounds a 375-acre lake and is one of south Georgia's major boating and water skiing sites. It includes camping and mini-golf facilities. *FYI:* Adel; (912) 896-3551. **John Tanner State Park** has two lakes for boating and fishing, plus the largest swim-ming beach in Georgia's state park system. *FYI:* 354 Tanner Beach Rd., Carrollton; (404) 830-2222.

The Cloister Resort on Sea Island has received world-wide acclaim for its facilities and excellent service

Brunswick and the Golden Isles Visitors Bureau

Watching Wildlife

Some of North America's most colorful birds live or stop over in Georgia. The 350 species sighted include colorful painted buntings, summer tanagers, cardinals, pileated woodpeckers, and yellow-throated warblers. Many wildlife management areas have developed nature trails and bird watching areas.

Okefenokee National Wildlife Refuge: This 438,000-acre refuge is a haven for everything from the endangered American alligator and the bald eagle to black bear and bobcat. Facilities include, a boardwalk, an observation tower, and nature trails; guided boat tours and overnight wilderness canoe trips are offered. *FYI:* 11 miles south of Folkston; (912) 496-3331.

Georgia Dept. of Industry and Trade

Okefenokee is the largest National Wildlife Refuge in the eastern United States

Piedmont National Wildlife Refuge: Deer, turkey, and the red-cockaded woodpecker can be seen along interpretive trails in the 35,000-acre refuge. Nearby **Bond Swamp National Wildlife Refuge** is a 5,000-acre habitat for American bald eagles. *FYI:* Piedmont National Wildlife Refuge, Round Oak; (912) 986-5441.

Savannah National Wildlife Refuge: One of the nation's oldest refuges began as a rice plantation. Dikes built by slave labor attract a variety of herons, egrets, bitterns, and wintering waterfowl. Savannah also administers Blackbeard, Wassaw, Wolf Island, and Harris Neck Wildlife Refuges. *FYI:* (912) 652-4415.

Blackbeard Island: Loggerhead turtles and alligators, and flocks of sanderlings, oystercatchers, and black skimmers congregate at Blackbeard's former hide-out. *FYI:* Access is by boat.

Harris Neck: Because of the area's great variety of species, including painted buntings and northern parulas, the Audubon Society holds annual bird counts here. *FYI:* 43 miles south of Savannah on Route 131.

Wolf Island: Clapper rails, herons, egrets, brown pelicans, and loggerhead turtles use the refuge. Closed to public use, except for saltwater fishing, crabbing, and shrimping.

Horsin' Around

Between 1865 and 1910, four **Barnesville** companies mass produced buggies, with one firm manufacturing 11,000 per year. Each September, **Barnesville Buggy Days** draws 60,000 people to watch antique buggy road races and other events. *FYI:* Barnesville Chamber of Commerce; (404) 358-2732. While

The Hawkinsville Harness Race features horse drawn sulkies

Barnesville bills itself as the "Buggy Capital of the World," **Hawkinsville** is the "Harness Horse Training Capital of the South." The annual training takes place on mile and half-mile tracks. The **Columbus Steeplechase** is part of the Sport of Kings Challenge and attracts more than 12,000 people to Callaway Gardens each November. *FYI:* Columbus; (706) 324-6252. **Augusta's Cutting Horse Futurity and Festival**, in January, is the East's largest skilled horse competitive event.

Competitors race from Helen to the coast in the Atlantic Ocean Balloon Race

Events

Flag City Shootout: The world's largest softball tournament draws 700 teams to Macon's Central City Park during the last weekend in April. *FYI:* (800) 768-3401.
Annual Masters Water Ski Tournament: The world's top competitors gather at Callaway Gardens in May for tricks, slaloms, and jumping. *FYI:* (800) 282-8181.
Belle Meade Fox Hunt: The event begins with a formal Blessing of the Hounds on the first Saturday in November, and continues every Wednesday and Saturday through March. A tractor-pulled "tally-ho" wagon affords glimpses of dogs chasing foxes while following through the hound country.

SPIRIT OF GEORGIA

Spanish and English explorers, pirates, gold miners, artists, and American Revolution and Civil War soldiers have all left their mark on Georgia. They have created part of its unique folklore and history, made discoveries which have benefited humanity, and interpreted the good and bad of the Georgia experience.

Thus, after 200 years, Georgia's spirit is an amalgamation of the poet, the working man, the rogue, and the idealist. It is a spirit tied to the rich red land, bound in tradition, and tempered by time.

Healthy Waters

1) Cave Spring: Each day the spring pumps 3 to 4 million gallons of water (at a constant 57 degrees) into a reflecting pool and shallow wading stream. A 1.5-acre mineral water swimming pool is one of the largest in Georgia. Guided tours of the 300,000-year-old cave's stalagmites and rock formations are available. *FYI:* Rolater Park, Cave Spring; (404) 777-8439.

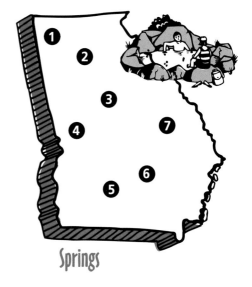

Springs

2) Lithia Springs: In the 1800s, doctors hailed the waters' curative properties and made the town a popular health spa—a summer resort for southerners and a wintering area for northerners. Lithia Springs Mineral Water Company now bottles the water and operates the Family Doctor Museum and Medicinal Garden. *FYI:* Lithia Springs; (404) 944-3880.

3) Indian Springs State Park: Indians used the springs' medicinal waters to heal their sick. In 1820 and 1825 the Creeks signed treaties here relinquishing all their lands in Georgia to the U.S. government. One of the nation's oldest state parks, Indian Springs offers camping, swimming, fishing, boating, and cottages near a 105-acre beach and lake. *FYI:* 678 Lake Clark Rd., Flovilla;

(404) 775-7241. Nearby **Historic Indian Springs Hotel** was built in 1823 by Chief William McIntosh, leader of the Lower Creek nation. It contains the only authentic 1800s-style flower, rose, and herb garden in the Southeast. *FYI:* (404) 775-6734.

4) Warm Springs: By the 1880s the area was a popular vacation destination for southern aristocrats. The pools still bubble year-round at 88 degrees and feed a fountain on the grounds of Franklin D. Roosevelt's Little White House. The Roosevelt Warm Springs Institute for Rehabilitation provides medical and vocational rehabilitation services to more than 3,000 people per year. *FYI:* Chamber of Commerce; (800) 532-1690.

5) Radium Springs: Water stays at a constant 68 degrees and gushes at 70,000 gallons per minute from Georgia's largest natural spring. A sandy beach borders the picturesque swimming spot, and southern pine, moss-draped live oak, and giant cypress trees shade the terraced rim. The restaurant retains a unique interior decor from its days as a 1920s club casino. Spring and summer swimming. *FYI:* 2500 Radium Springs Rd., Albany; (912) 889-0244.

6) Jay Bird Springs: Enjoy the mineral waters in Georgia's oldest swimming pool, play miniature golf, or skate on a rink. Cabins and camping are available. *FYI:* 12 miles south of Eastman; (912) 868-2728.

7) Magnolia Springs State Park: The springs' crystal clear waters are situated on the site of Camp Lawton, a Confederate prison camp built in 1864 to relieve the crowding at Andersonville. About 10,000 prisoners were held here. *FYI:* Millen; (912) 982-1660.

Medical Miracles

The **Medical College of Georgia**, built in 1835, was Georgia's first medical school and one of the first in America. The building is considered a prime example of Greek Revival style architecture. *FYI:* 598 Telfair St., Augusta; (706) 721-7238.

Dr. Crawford W. Long

Dr. Crawford W. Long, born in Danielsville, made medical history on March 30, 1842, when he was the first physician to use ether as an anesthesia. He charged $2 for the operation and 25 cents for the ether, but he didn't bother promoting or patenting his discovery. Due to primitive communications and the isolation of communities, word of his procedure spread slowly. The **Crawford W. Long Museum**, the site of his first painless surgery, contains some of his early anesthesia equipment. *FYI:* 28 College St., Jefferson; (706) 367-5307.

Dr. Robert Battey, a pharmacist and doctor, practiced medicine in Europe and as a Confederate Army surgeon. In 1869 he performed the first ovarian operation for therapeutic reasons. He was born in Augusta and practiced in Rome, Georgia.

Numerous parks, town squares, and historic cemeteries display Confederate monuments

Historic Cemeteries

Many Georgia cemeteries contain graves of Union and Confederate soldiers. Some that mark the final resting place of famous people and statesmen include:

Rose Hill Cemetery: One of the nation's oldest surviving public cemetery parks dates to 1839. Listed on the National Register of Historic Places, its interments include 600 Confederate and Union soldiers, and late Allman

Brothers Band members Duane Allman and Berry Oakley. *FYI:* 1091 Riverside Dr., Macon; (912) 751-9119.

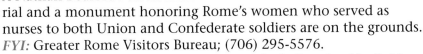

Myrtle Hill Cemetery: Hundreds of Confederate and Federal soldiers; Ellen Axson Wilson, wife of President Woodrow Wilson; the Known Soldier; and Dr. Robert Battey are buried here. A Nathan Bedford Forrest memorial and a monument honoring Rome's women who served as nurses to both Union and Confederate soldiers are on the grounds. *FYI:* Greater Rome Visitors Bureau; (706) 295-5576.

Historic Oakland Cemetery: Margaret Mitchell and golfer Bobby Jones are buried amidst a treasure trove of Victorian funeral statuary. *FYI:* 248 Oakland Ave., S.E., Atlanta; (404) 577-8163.

Oak Grove Cemetery: The cemetery was included in the original St. Marys town plat of 1788. Settlers and soldiers of every war are buried here. Some tombstones have French inscriptions of Acadian settlers from Nova Scotia. *FYI:* St. Marys.

Bonaventure: In one of the nation's most photographed riverfront gardens, 200-year-old live oak trees shade the graves of Savannah statesmen, citizens, and soldiers. *FYI:* Bonaventure Rd., Savannah.

Colonial Park: The cemetery was in use from 1750 to 1853 and contains the grave of Button Gwinnett, a signer of the Declaration of Independence. *FYI:* Oglethorpe and Abercorn Sts., Savannah.

The Man Who Was Buried Three Times

Charles Graves was killed in World War I and buried in France in 1918. To symbolize the tragedy of war and attempt to prevent it in the future, he was chosen as America's "Known Soldier." His body was exhumed, shipped to his hometown, and buried again in Rome's Antioch Cemetery. Some felt the site was not prominent enough or easily accessible to the public. Others threatened to file an injunction to prevent a third burial. On the night of September 11, 1923, American Legionnaires moved the coffin to Myrtle Hill Cemetery, which had been designated a memorial park for World War I veterans, and he was buried a third time.

Spooky Places

According to legend, when an itinerant minister was refused permission to preach in Augusta's Lower Market, he declared that the marketplace would be destroyed. In 1878 a cyclone leveled the building except for one Doric pillar. Years later, when workers attempted to move it, they were struck by lightning. The **Haunted Pillar** still stands. *FYI:* 5th at Broad, Augusta.

Georgia Dept. of Industry and Trade

According to legend, the Mackay House, built in Augusta in 1760, is haunted by 13 Americans who were hanged there during the American Revolution

Dell-Goodall House survived the curse of another itinerant preacher. In 1830 a traveling evangelist came to Jacksonboro to conduct services. Townspeople considered him an eccentric and refused to give him shelter. Finally the Goodalls took him into their home, and he spent the night. The next morning townspeople warned him never to return. The evangelist cursed everything except the Goodalls and their home. After the town lost the county seat in 1847, it was deserted; only the Goodall home remains. *FYI:* Near Sylvania.

In **Dalton**, a Cherokee Indian chief named Redbird is buried near the railroad tracks. His spirit supposedly haunts the railroad, and many train wrecks have occurred in the area. *FYI:* 715 N. Chattanooga Ave., Dalton; (706) 272-7676.

Cargoes of slaves were frequently unloaded at **Ebo's Landing** on St. Simons Island. The Ebo, a Nigerian tribe, resisted and were led into the ocean by their leader, who believed that the waters which had brought them to these shores would take them back to their native land. They drowned, and it is said that their spirits still inhabit the area.

Lighthouses

Tybee Island Lighthouse is Georgia's oldest and tallest lighthouse and one of the first public structures in the state. In 1736 General Oglethorpe had the first navigational aid erected near the present lighthouse. A second tower, constructed in 1742 and lighted in 1748, was the third lighthouse built in America. The present 154-

foot-high structure was rebuilt in 1887. Guided tours are available, and visitors can climb to the top for sweeping views of the countryside. *FYI:* 18 miles east of Savannah; (912) 786-5801.

St. Simons Lighthouse, the oldest brick building in the area was built in 1872 and is still maintained as an operating light by the U.S. Coast Guard. The lighthouse and Museum of Coastal History, in the keeper's cottage, contains artifacts and exhibits. Some 129 steps lead to a panoramic view of the surrounding seascape. *FYI:* (912) 638-4666.

St. Simons Lighthouse and Museum

Brunswick and The Golden Isles Visitors Bureau

Star Gazing

Fernbank Science Center: One of nation's largest planetariums is surrounded by gardens and a 65-acre old-growth hardwood forest. *FYI:* 767 Clifton Rd., N.E., Atlanta; (404) 378-4311.

Museum of Arts and Sciences: The Mark Smith Planetarium, one of Georgia's largest, interprets the universe with an observatory and daily star shows featuring lasers and Quadraphonic sound. *FYI:* 4182 Forsyth Rd., Macon; (912) 477-3232.

Covered Bridges

Covered bridges are romantic reminders of Georgia's horse-and-buggy past. They served multiple purposes over and above spanning streams. Outlaws used them as concealment while awaiting victims, liquor was stored in them during prohibition, and they sometimes served as secret rendezvous for lovers. The addition of a roof doubled a bridge's life span.

Stovall covered bridge is one of 18 covered bridges in Georgia

Watson Mill Bridge State Park: The four spans of Georgia's longest covered bridge stretch 236 feet across the south fork of the Broad River. The century-old bridge is held together with wooden pins rather than nails. *FYI:* Comer; (404) 783-5349.

Stovall Covered Bridge: Featured in the movie *I'd Climb the Highest Mountain*, the 35-foot-long, one lane bridge was built around 1895. Its Kingpost truss, containing a centerpost connected by diagonal posts anchored to baseboards, is one of the earliest covered bridge designs dating to at least 1570. *FYI:* GA 255 north of Sautee.

Lowery Covered Bridge: Georgia's oldest covered bridge has a lattice design. Its timbers were numbered when it was dismantled and moved to its present site. *FYI:* Six miles from Cartersville via GA 113.

Auchumpkee Covered Bridge: The Town Lattice style bridge was built in 1893. *FYI:* 12 miles south of Thomaston on Allen Rd.

Big Red Oak Creek Bridge: The 116-foot-long bridge of Town Lattice design was built around 1840. *FYI:* Four miles north of Woodbury.

Golden History

Several Georgia sites interpret local gold mining history and offer recreational gold panning. At **Crisson's Gold Mine** you can pan and keep any gold you find. *FYI:* Dahlonega; (706) 864-6363.

Consolidated Mines was once the largest mining operation east of the Mississippi. Although it ceased mining operations in the 1930s, tours of the facility and recreational gold panning continue to be offered. *FYI:* One mile east of Dahlonega; (706) 684-3711. Every method of historic gold mining occurred at the Bavarian-style village of **Helen**. At the town's **Historic Gold Mines**, visitors can pan, mine, and dredge for gold. *FYI:* (706) 878-3052.

Recreational gold panning at Dahlonega's Blackburn Park

Lost Treasure

Chennault Plantation, built in 1853, may have played an important part in a gold train robbery. The Confederate treasury was attacked and robbed, and the money reportedly was last seen at the plantation. Legend has it that it is still buried somewhere on the grounds. *FYI:* Drive by only, Lincolnton area.

Historic Mills

Chappell's Mill: Built in 1811 and saved from destruction by Sherman in 1864, it uses an original dam which floods 75 acres.

At John's Mill, in Talking Rock, visitors can watch the water-powered grist mill grind corn, wheat, and rye and purchase the meal it grinds

The mill grinds 15,000 bushels of corn per year by the old process of dry milling on a 100-year-old grinding stone. *FYI:* 13 miles north of Dublin; (912) 272-5128.

George L. Smith State Park: An 1880 mill and mill house and a covered bridge are attractions. *FYI:* GA Hwy. 23, four miles S.E. of Twin City; (912) 763-2759.

One and Onlys

The Double-Barreled Cannon

Athens' double-barreled cannon

Athens owns a one-of-a-kind Civil War relic. The double-barreled cannon was invented in 1863 and cast at the Athens Foundry and Machine Works. Each barrel was loaded with a cannon ball connected by an eight-foot chain. In theory the balls were supposed to fly out, draw the chain taut, and kill everything in their path. Because the firing was not synchronized, the balls shot through the air in a circular motion, demolishing parts of a cornfield and small trees. The chain broke, and the balls went in separate directions, one killing a cow and the other damaging a log cabin's chimney. A line of poles—the designated target—stood untouched. *FYI:* Cannon Park at City Hall, Athens.

The Tree That Owns Itself

Colonel William H. Jackson, a University of Georgia professor, enjoyed the shade of one of his white oak trees. In 1820 he registered a deed which read ". . . does convey unto the said oak tree, entire possession of itself and of the land within eight feet of it on all sides." During the 1940s the original tree fell in a windstorm and a second tree grew from one of its acorns. No one is sure that the tree actually owns itself, because nobody has ever challenged the deed. *FYI:* Corner of Dearing and Finley Sts., Athens.

Marble Mania

Although Georgia has long been a leading producer of granite and marble, relatively few buildings in the state are made of these stones. **Emmanuel Episcopal Church**, a Victorian Gothic structure, was built in 1899 of Georgia granite. *FYI:* 185 Prince Ave., Athens. The **Tate House**, known as the Pink Marble Mansion, was built in 1926 by Colonel Sam Tate, president of the Georgia Marble Company, to display marble from his quarries. The house and 27-acre estate now serve as a bed and breakfast inn. *FYI:* Tate. The **Georgia Marble Festival**, held in Jasper the first weekend in October, includes Georgia Marble Company and mine tours. *FYI:* (706) 692-5600.

Georgia Dept. of Industry and Trade

The **Lithonia Granite Festival**, in July, celebrates local granite heritage with quarrying demonstrations and local mining company exhibits. *FYI:* Lithonia; (404) 482-1808.

Superlatives

In 1977 former Coca-Cola president **Robert Woodruff** made the largest single gift in the history of American philanthropy when he gave $105 million to Atlanta's Emory University. **Macon City Auditorium** has the world's largest copper dome. It stretches 152 feet in diameter. *FYI:* Cherry & First Sts., Macon.

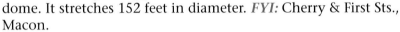

The I.T.T. Rayonier plant in **Jesup** is the world's largest chemical cellulose-producing pulp mill. **Carrollton** has the world's largest privately owned rod and cable manufacturing company. And Sony Music built the world's largest audio and video cassette manufacturing factory in Carrollton.

Fayette County Courthouse, built in 1825, is the oldest continually used courthouse in Georgia. *FYI:* 200 Courthouse Sq., Fayetteville; (404) 461-6041.

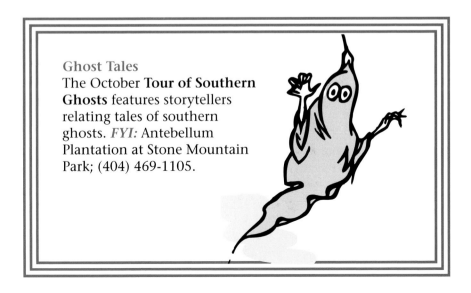

Ghost Tales

The October **Tour of Southern Ghosts** features storytellers relating tales of southern ghosts. *FYI:* Antebellum Plantation at Stone Mountain Park; (404) 469-1105.

KIDS' ADVENTURES

Attractions Galore

Atlanta Beach Sports and Entertainment Complex: A 100-acre water and recreation park offers a white sand beach, a spring-fed lake with a kids' pool, and a raceway. *FYI:* 2474 Walt Stephens Rd., Jonesboro; (404) 478-1932.

Discovery Zone: Indoor playgrounds are designed for children 12 and under and include a mountain to climb and obstacle courses. *FYI:* I-85 Exit 40, 1630 Pleasant Hill Rd., Duluth, (404) 923-8889; and 4400 Roswell Rd., Marietta, (404) 565-5699.

Fernbank Museum of Natural History: The "Georgia Adventure" section appeals to 6- to 10-year-olds, while "Fantasy Forest" is designed for 3- to 5-year-olds. *FYI:* 767 Clifton Rd., N.E., Atlanta; (404) 370-0960.

On a Savannah safari, parents and children try to identify architectural animals from wrought iron egrets, gargoyles, and other animals

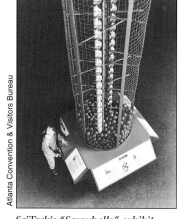

SciTrek's "Screwballs" exhibit

Krystal River Water Park: The complex includes seven water slides, a kiddie pool with three slides, a miniature golf course, and an arcade. *FYI:* 799 Industrial Park Dr., Evans; (706) 855-0061.

Savannah Science Museum: Hands-on exhibits in natural history, astronomy, and science are featured along with displays on natural and physical sciences, and prehistoric animals of the Georgia coast. Planetarium shows and a solar energy robot are also highlighted. *FYI:* Paulsen and 62nd Sts., Savannah; (912) 355-6705.

Six Flags Over Georgia: The 331 acres and more than 100 thrill rides include roller coasters, eight fantasy-themed amusement parks, four water rides, kiddie shows, and musical extravaganzas. *FYI:* Six Flags Exit off I-20; (404) 948-9290.

SciTrek: The Science and Technology Museum of Atlanta is one of the nation's top ten physical science museums. More than 100 interactive exhibits illustrate basic principals of science. Main halls interpret electricity and magnetism, light, color and perception, simple machines, and mathematics. Kidspace is reserved for kids ages 2 to 7. *FYI:* 395 Piedmont Ave., Atlanta; (404) 522-5500.

Ridin' the roller coaster at Six Flags Over Georgia

Stone Mountain: Offers family camping, lakes and beaches, wildlife trails, skylift rides to the rock's top, train rides, paddlewheel river boats, an antique auto museum, and laser shows. *FYI:* Stone Mountain Park; (404) 498-5690.

Joel Chandler Harris (1848–1908)

Harris, who was born in Eatonton, worked on several Georgia newspapers. In 1878, at the suggestion of the *Atlanta Constitution*'s editor, he began writing a daily column of humorous sketches. The result was several volumes of Uncle Remus stories, which chronicled the adventures of the Tar Baby and Brer Rabbit, Fox, and B'ar. The stories were based on tales a former slave told to children who visited his cabin. Harris' use of black characters and dialect was a unique contribution to American literature. His Queen Anne Victorian-era home, **The Wren's Nest**, is a National Historic Landmark containing books and Brer Rabbit memorabilia. *FYI:* 1050 Ralph David Abernathy Blvd. S.W., Atlanta; (404) 753-7735. Eatonton's **Brer Rabbit Statue** and **Uncle Remus Museum and Park** honor his work. The museum is part of the home of Joseph Sidney Turner, who was the prototype for the little boy in the Uncle Remus stories. It recalls the slave cabin setting and houses a Disney portrait of Uncle Remus and the little boy, wood carvings of the critters, and first editions of Harris' works. *FYI:* U.S. 441, Eatonton; (404) 485-6856.

Zoos, Museums, and More

Babyland General Hospital's Cabbage Patch Kids

American Adventures: Created for children under 12, the turn-of-the-century theme park offers go-carts, miniature golf, a mini roller coaster, a carousel, and an arcade. *FYI:* I-75, Exit 133, Marietta; (404) 424-9283. Next door, **White Water** has family raft rides, Atlanta's only ocean wave pool, and the four-story Tree House Island. *FYI:* 250 North Cobb Pkwy.; (404) 424-9283.

Babyland General Hospital: This 1900 medical clinic is the birthplace and home of the famous Cabbage Patch Kids. Visitors can watch the "birth" of an original kid, and doctors and nurses are on-hand to find a suitable match for those interested in adopting. *FYI:* Cleveland; (706) 865-2171.

Center For Puppetry Arts: Productions at the nation's largest puppetry center have included dinosaur shows, fairy tales, and African folk tales. *FYI:* 1404 Spring St. at 18th, Atlanta; (404) 873-3089.

Chehaw Wild Animal Park: Black bears, bobcats, bison, and other animals roam free in this zoo. *FYI:* Philema Rd., Albany; (912) 430-5275.

Cloudland Canyon: Whimsical Fairyland Caverns and Mother Goose Village offer enchanting interpretations of fairy tales. *FYI:* 1400 Patten Rd., Lookout Mountain; (706) 820-2531.

Mary Miller Doll Museum: One of the Southeast's largest doll museums displays some 3,000 dolls, including 1840 chinaheads and dolls made by master artisans. *FYI:* 1523 Glynn Ave., Brunswick; (912) 267-7569.

Museum of the Hills: Lifestyles of hill-country people are depicted in wax. Also includes a "fantasy kingdom" of fairy tales. *FYI:* Helen; (706) 878-3140.

National Science Center: Created by the U.S. Army and the National Science

Callaway Gardens offers activities for children as well as adults

Center Foundation, prototypes illustrate sound waves, magnetism, lasers, electricity, and mathematics. Visitors can participate in science demonstrations and attend STARLAB portable planetarium presentations. *FYI:* Fort Gordon; (706) 791-7680.

Noah's Ark: Pre-arranged tours are conducted at the nation's only facility to treat and house more than 600 common and exotic animals that have been injured, abandoned, or condemned. *FYI:* 1425 Locust Grove Rd., Locust Grove; (404) 957-0888.

Oakleigh: Sherman's former headquarters have been converted into a museum housing more than 1,500 dolls. *FYI:* Wall St., Calhoun; (706) 629-1515.

Pine Mountain Wild Animal Park: Drive or take a tour bus through 500 acres, where hundreds of species roam free. Visit the serpentorium, alligator pit, monkey house, and petting zoo. *FYI:* 1300 Oak Grove Rd., Pine Mountain; (706) 663-8744; outside Georgia, (800) 367-2751.

Skidaway Marine Science Complex: A 12,000-gallon aquarium plus displays of coastal archaeological finds are part of the oceanographic center. *FYI:* Skidaway Island Dr., Savannah; (912) 356-2496.

Summer Waves: The 11-acre water park boasts an "endless" river and a slow-motion ocean. Other attractions include an inner tube flume, Pirate's Passage flumes, four-story-high serpentine slides, and a children's pool. *FYI:* S. Riverview Dr., Jekyll Island; (912) 635-2074.

Rare Sumatran tigers are part of Zoo Atlanta's "Ketambe" exhibit

Zoo Atlanta: The 37-acre park is known for its collection of reptiles and 900 other animals, which roam natural habitats simulating Okefenokee Swamp, Great Savannah, the African rain forest, and the Arctic tundra. *FYI:* Grant Park, 800 Cherokee Ave., S.E., Atlanta; (404) 624-5678.

Festival

At the **Rock City Fairy Tale Festival**, in August, fairy tale characters such as Little Red Riding Hood and Sleeping Beauty mingle and entertain along with storytellers, puppeteers, clowns, and magicians. *FYI:* Lookout Mountain; (706) 820-2531.

INDEX

Other Books from John Muir Publications

Travel Books by Rick Steves
Asia Through the Back Door, 4th ed., 400 pp. $16.95
Europe 101: History, Art, and Culture for the Traveler, 5th ed., 368 pp. $17.95
Mona Winks: Self-Guided Tours of Europe's Top Museums, 3rd ed., 496 pp. $19.95
Rick Steves' Best of the Baltics and Russia, 144 pp. $9.95
Rick Steves' Best of Europe, 544 pp. $16.95
Rick Steves' Best of France, Belgium, and the Netherlands, 240 pp. $12.95
Rick Steves' Best of Germany, Austria, and Switzerland, 240 pp. $12.95
Rick Steves' Best of Great Britain, 192 pp. $11.95
Rick Steves' Best of Italy, 208 pp. $11.95
Rick Steves' Best of Scandinavia, 192 pp. $11.95
Rick Steves' Best of Spain and Portugal, 192 pp. $11.95
Rick Steves' Europe Through the Back Door, 13th ed., 480 pp. $17.95
Rick Steves' French Phrase Book, 2nd ed., 176 pp. $4.95
Rick Steves' German Phrase Book, 2nd ed., 176 pp. $4.95
Rick Steves' Italian Phrase Book, 2nd ed., 176 pp. $4.95
Rick Steves' Spanish and Portuguese Phrase Book, 2nd ed., 304 pp. $5.95
Rick Steves' French/German/Italian Phrase Book, 320 pp. $6.95

A Natural Destination Series
Belize: A Natural Destination, 3rd ed., 336 pp. $16.95
Costa Rica: A Natural Destination, 3rd ed., 400 pp. $17.95
Guatemala: A Natural Destination, 2nd ed., 336 pp. $16.95

Undiscovered Islands Series
Undiscovered Islands of the Caribbean, 4th ed., 288 pp. $16.95
Undiscovered Islands of the Mediterranean, 2nd ed., 256 pp. $13.95

Undiscovered Islands of the U.S. and Canadian West Coast, 288 pp. $12.95

For Birding Enthusiasts
The Birder's Guide to Bed and Breakfasts: U.S. and Canada, 2nd ed., 416 pp. $17.95
The Visitor's Guide to the Birds of the Central National Parks: U.S. and Canada, 400 pp. $15.95
The Visitor's Guide to the Birds of the Eastern National Parks: U.S. and Canada, 400 pp. $15.95
The Visitor's Guide to the Birds of the Rocky Mountain National Parks: U.S. and Canada, 432 pp. $15.95

Unique Travel Series
Each is 112 pages and $10.95 paper.
Unique Arizona
Unique California
Unique Colorado
Unique Florida
Unique Georgia
Unique New England
Unique New Mexico
Unique Texas
Unique Washington

2 to 22 Days Itinerary Planners
2 to 22 Days in the American Southwest, 192 pp. $11.95
2 to 22 Days in Asia, 192 pp. $10.95
2 to 22 Days in Australia, 192 pp. $11.95
2 to 22 Days in California, 192 pp. $11.95
2 to 22 Days in Eastern Canada, 240 pp $11.95
2 to 22 Days in Florida, 192 pp. $11.95
2 to 22 Days Around the Great Lakes, 192 pp. $11.95
2 to 22 Days in Hawaii, 192 pp. $11.95
2 to 22 Days in New England, 192 pp. $11.95
2 to 22 Days in New Zealand, 192 pp. $11.95
2 to 22 Days in the Pacific Northwest, 192 pp. $11.95
2 to 22 Days in the Rockies, 192 pp. $11.95

2 to 22 Days in Texas, 192 pp. $11.95

2 to 22 Days in Thailand, 192 pp. $10.95

22 Days Around the World, 264 pp. $13.95

Other Terrific Travel Titles

The 100 Best Small Art Towns in America, 224 pp. $12.95

The Big Book of Adventure Travel, 384 pp. $17.95

Elderhostels: The Students' Choice, 2nd ed., 304 pp. $15.95

Environmental Vacations: Volunteer Projects to Save the Planet, 2nd ed., 248 pp. $16.95

A Foreign Visitor's Guide to America, 224 pp. $12.95

Great Cities of Eastern Europe, 256 pp. $16.95

Indian America: A Traveler's Companion, 4th ed., 480 pp. $18.95

Interior Furnishings Southwest, 256 pp. $19.95

Opera! The Guide to Western Europe's Great Houses, 296 pp. $18.95

Paintbrushes and Pistols: How the Taos Artists Sold the West, 288 pp. $17.95

The People's Guide to Mexico, 10th ed., 608 pp. $18.95

Ranch Vacations: The Complete Guide to Guest and Resort, Fly-Fishing, and Cross-Country Skiing Ranches, 3rd ed., 512 pp. $19.95

The Shopper's Guide to Art and Crafts in the Hawaiian Islands, 272 pp. $13.95

The Shopper's Guide to Mexico, 224 pp. $9.95

Understanding Europeans, 272 pp. $14.95

A Viewer's Guide to Art: A Glossary of Gods, People, and Creatures, 144 pp. $10.95

Watch It Made in the U.S.A.: A Visitor's Guide to the Companies that Make Your Favorite Products, 272 pp. $16.95

Parenting Titles

Being a Father: Family, Work, and Self, 176 pp. $12.95

Preconception: A Woman's Guide to Preparing for Pregnancy and Parenthood, 232 pp. $14.95

Schooling at Home: Parents, Kids, and Learning, 264 pp., $14.95

Teens: A Fresh Look, 240 pp. $14.95

Automotive Titles

The Greaseless Guide to Car Care 2nd ed., 272 pp. $19.95

How to Keep Your Datsun/Nissan Alive, 544 pp. $21.95

How to Keep Your Subaru Alive, 480 pp. $21.95

How to Keep Your Toyota Pickup Alive, 392 pp. $21.95

How to Keep Your VW Alive, 16th ed., 464 pp. $25

Ordering Information

Please check your local bookstore for our books, or call **1-800-888-7504** to order direct. All orders are shipped via UPS; see chart below to calculate your shipping charge for U.S. destinations. **No post office boxes please; we must have a street address to ensure delivery.** If the book you request is not available, we will hold your check until we can ship it. Foreign orders will be shipped surface rate unless otherwise requested; please enclose $3 for the first item and $1 for each additional item.

For U.S. Orders Totaling	Add
Up to $15.00	$4.25
$15.01 to $45.00	$5.25
$45.01 to $75.00	$6.25
$75.01 or more	$7.25

Methods of Payment

Check, money order, American Express, MasterCard, or Visa. We cannot be responsible for cash sent through the mail. For credit card orders, include your card number, expiration date, and your signature, or call **1-800-888-7504**. American Express card orders can only be shipped to billing address of cardholder. Sorry, no C.O.D.'s. Residents of sunny New Mexico, add 6.25% tax to total.

Address all orders and inquiries to:
John Muir Publications
P.O. Box 613
Santa Fe, NM 87504
(505) 982-4078
(800) 888-7504